S0-BIW-501

WITHDRAWN

War in the Persian Gulf
Primary Sources

From Operation Desert Storm to Operation Iraqi Freedom

War in the Persian Gulf Primary Sources

From Operation Desert Storm to Operation Iraqi Freedom

LAURIE COLLIER HILLSTROM

Julie Carnagie,
Project Editor

U·X·L

*An imprint of Thomson Gale,
a part of The Thomson Corporation*

Detroit • New York • San Francisco • San Diego • New Haven, Conn. • Waterville, Maine • London • Munich

LONGWOOD PUBLIC LIBRARY

War in the Persian Gulf Primary Sources: From Operation Desert Storm to Operation Iraqi Freedom

Laurie Collier Hillstrom

Project Editor
Julie L. Carnagie

Permissions
Shalice Shah-Caldwell

Imaging and Multimedia
Lezlie Light, Michael Logusz, Kelly A. Quin, Leitha Etheridge-Sims

Product Design
Pamela Galbreath

Composition
Evi Seoud

Manufacturing
Rita Wimberley

©2004 by U•X•L. U•X•L is an imprint of Thomson Gale, a division of Thomson Learning, Inc.

U•X•L® is a registered trademark used herein under license. Thomson Learning™ is a trademark used herein under license.

For more information, contact:
Thomson Gale
27500 Drake Rd.
Farmington Hills, MI 48331-3535
Or you can visit our Internet site at
http://www.gale.com

ALL RIGHTS RESERVED
No part of this work covered by the copyright hereon may be reproduced or used in any form or by any means—graphic, electronic, or mechanical, including photocopying, recording, taping, Web distribution, or information storage retrieval systems—without the written permission of the publisher.

For permission to use material from this product, submit your request via Web at http://www.gale-edit.com/permissions, or you may download our Permissions Request form and submit your request by fax or mail to:

Permissions Department
Thomson Gale
27500 Drake Rd.
Farmington Hills, MI 48331-3535
Permissions Hotline:
248-699-8006 or 800-877-4253, ext. 8006
Fax: 248-699-8074 or 800-762-4058

Cover photographs reproduced by permission of AP/Wide World, (George H. W. Bush, Anne Garrels), and Archive Photos, Inc. (Saddam Hussein).

While every effort has been made to ensure the reliability of the information presented in this publication, Thomson Gale does not guarantee the accuracy of the data contained herein. Thomson Gale accepts no payment for listing; and inclusion in the publication of any organization, agency, institution, publication, service, or individual does not imply endorsement by the editors or publisher. Errors brought to the attention of the publisher and verified to the satisfaction of the publisher will be corrected in future editions.

Library of Congress Control Number: 2004004105

Printed in the United States of America
10 9 8 7 6 5 4 3 2 1

ISBN 0-7876-9088-0

This title is also available as an e-book. ISBN 0-7876-9347-2
Contact your Gale sales representative for ordering information.

Contents

Reader's Guide

*W*ar *in the Persian Gulf Primary Sources: From Operation Desert Storm to Operation Iraqi Freedom* presents tweleve full or excerpted documents related to the U.S.-led wars against Iraq that took place in 1991 and 2003. These documents range from notable speeches that mark important points in the conflicts to personal diaries and letters that reflect the hopes, dreams, fears, and experiences of ordinary soldiers and civilians. The excerpts are arranged chronologically, beginning with Iraqi leader Saddam Hussein's decision to invade Kuwait in 1990 and ending with an Iraqi citizen's 2003 Internet diary describing conditions in Baghdad under U.S. occupation.

Some of the selections discuss highly personal issues, such as a U.S. soldier's participation in the 1991 ground assault and a Muslim teenager's experiences with prejudice in American society. Others chronicle major events associated with the Persian Gulf Wars, like the start of the 1991 air war or the fall of Baghdad to U.S. troops in 2003. Furthermore, the works included in this volume present a wide range of perspectives on the conflicts. For example, some entries provide insights into the feelings of Iraqi citizens and Middle

Eastern leaders. Others provide a closer look at U.S. military strategies and the goals of American political leaders.

Included are excerpts from Iraqi President Saddam Hussein's controversial 1990 meeting with U.S. Ambassador to Iraq April Glaspie; CNN reporter Peter Arnett's famous 1991 coverage of the first night of bombing from a Baghdad hotel; U.S. General H. Norman Schwarzkopf's description of the successful 1991 coalition ground war strategy; and former U.S. national security advisor Brent Scowcroft's 2002 editorial "Don't Attack Saddam."

Format

Each excerpt included in *War in the Persian Gulf Primary Sources: From Operation Desert Storm to Operation Iraqi Freedom* features the following additional text:

- **Introductory material** places the document and its author in historical context.

- **Things to remember while reading** offers readers important background information and directs them to central ideas in the text.

- **Excerpt** presents the document in its original spelling and format.

- **What happened next...** discusses the impact of the document and provides an account of subsequent historical events.

- **Did you know...** provides interesting facts about the document and its author.

- **For More Information** offers resources for further study of the document and its author as well as sources used by the authors in writing the material.

Entries in *War in the Persian Gulf Primary Sources: From Operation Desert Storm to Operation Iraqi Freedom* include numerous sidebars, some focusing on the author of the featured document, others highlighting interesting, related information. Approximately sixty black-and-white photos illustrate the text, and each excerpt has a glossary that runs alongside the reprinted document to identify unfamiliar terms and ideas contained within the material. *War in the Persian Gulf Primary Sources: From Operation Desert Storm to Operation Iraqi*

Freedom also includes a timeline, a glossary, a "People to Know" section, sources for further reading, and a subject index.

War in the Persian Gulf Reference Library: From Operation Desert Storm to Operation Iraqi Freedom

War in the Persian Gulf Primary Sources: From Operation Desert Storm to Operation Iraqi Freedom is only one component of a three-volume War in the Persian Gulf Reference Library: From Operation Desert Storm to Operation Iraqi Freedom. The other two titles in this multivolume set include:

- *War in the Persian Gulf Almanac: From Operation Desert Storm to Operation Iraqi Freedom* presents a comprehensive overview of the 1991 and 2003 U.S.-led wars against Iraq. The volume's twelve chapters are arranged chronologically and cover all aspects of the two conflicts, from Iraq's 1990 invasion of Kuwait through the fall of Baghdad to U.S. forces in 2003. The *Almanac* begins by describing the history of the Middle East and Saddam Hussein's rise to power in Iraq and concludes by examining the complex issues involved in the transition to a democratic Iraqi government. More than sixty black-and-white photographs and maps help illustrate the text. Numerous sidebars highlight interesting individuals and facts. *War in the Persian Gulf Almanac: From Operation Desert Storm to Operation Iraqi Freedom* also includes a timeline of important events, a glossary, a "People to Know" section, research and activity ideas, sources for further reading, and an index.

- *War in the Persian Gulf Biographies: From Operation Desert Storm to Operation Iraqi Freedom* presents profiles of thirty men and women who participated in or were affected by the 1991 Persian Gulf War and the 2003 Iraq War. The volume covers such key people as political leaders George H. W. Bush, George W. Bush, Saddam Hussein, Yasir Arafat, Tony Blair, and Jacques Chirac; military leaders Colin Powell and H. Norman Schwarzkopf; journalists Christiane Amanpour, Peter Arnett, and Bob Simon; and prisoners of war Jeffrey Zaun and Jessica Lynch. The volume is filled with more than sixty black-and-white photographs, sidebars, and individual "Where to Learn More" sections. *War in the Persian Gulf Biographies: From Operation Desert Storm to Operation Iraqi Freedom* also includes a timeline of key events, a glossary, a "People to Know" section, sources for further reading, and an index.

• A cumulative index of all three titles in War in the Persian Gulf Reference Library: From Operations Desert Storm to Operation Iraqi Freedom is also available.

Advisors

A note of appreciation is extended to the *War in the Persian Gulf Primary Sources: From Operation Desert Storm to Operation Iraqi Freedom* advisors who provided invaluable suggestions when the work was in its formative stages:

Erik D. France
Librarian
University of Liggett Upper School
Grosse Pointe Woods, Michigan

Ann West LaPrise
Junior High/Elementary Librarian
Huron School District
New Boston, Michigan

Angela Leeper
Educational Consultant
Wake Forest, North Carolina

Comments and Suggestions

We welcome your comments on *War in the Persian Gulf Primary Sources: From Operation Desert Storm to Operation Iraqi Freedom* and suggestions for other topics in history to consider. Please write: Editors, *War in the Persian Gulf Primary Sources: From Operation Desert Storm to Operation Iraqi Freedom*, U•X•L, 27500 Drake Road, Farmington Hills, MI 48331-3535; call toll-free 800-877-4253; fax to 248-699-8097; or send e-mail via http://www.gale.com.

Timeline of Events

1922   British High Commissioner Sir Percy Cox establishes the borders of Iraq and Kuwait.

1927   British explorers make the largest oil strike in the world to date at Kirkuk in northern Iraq.

1932   Iraq gains its independence from British colonial rule.

1937   Saddam Hussein is born in a village near Tikrit, Iraq.

1961   Kuwait gains its independence from British colonial rule.

1968   The Baath Party takes control of the government of Iraq.

1979   Hussein becomes president of Iraq.

1979   The government of nearby Iran is overthrown by Islamic fundamentalists under the Ayatollah Khomeini.

1980   Iraq declares war against Iran.

1983   Iraq uses chemical weapons for the first time during the Iran-Iraq War.

1988   The Iran-Iraq War ends.

1988 Iraq uses chemical weapons against the Kurdish people of northern Iraq.

January 1989 George H.W. Bush is inaugurated the thirty-ninth president of the United States.

July 17, 1990 Hussein threatens to use force against Kuwait.

July 24, 1990 Tens of thousands of Iraqi troops begin gathering along the Kuwaiti border.

July 25, 1990 Hussein meets with April Glaspie, the U.S. ambassador to Iraq.

July 31, 1990 Iraqi and Kuwaiti officials meet in Jedda, Saudi Arabia, to discuss Iraq's concerns about border issues and oil prices.

August 2, 1990 Iraq invades Kuwait.

August 2, 1990 The United Nations (UN) Security Council passes Resolution 660, condemning Iraq's invasion of Kuwait.

August 6, 1990 The UN Security Council passes Resolution 661, imposing economic sanctions on Iraq.

August 6, 1990 Saudi Arabia agrees to allow American and other foreign troops into the country.

August 7, 1990 U.S. President George H. W. Bush begins sending American troops to Saudi Arabia for Operation Desert Shield.

August 8, 1990 Hussein announces the annexation of Kuwait by Iraq.

August 10, 1990 The UN Security Council passes Resolution 662, condemning Iraq's annexation of Kuwait.

August 15, 1990 Hussein makes peace with Iran by agreeing to all conditions of the 1988 cease-fire that ended the Iran-Iraq War.

August 18, 1990 Iraq announces that it plans to hold Westerners who had been in Iraq and Kuwait at the time of the invasion and use them as "human shields" at military targets.

September 1, 1990 Iraq begins releasing some Western women and children it had been holding hostage since the invasion.

September 9, 1990 U.S. President George H. W. Bush meets with Soviet President Mikhail Gorbachev at the Helsinki Summit; the two leaders reach agreement on a plan to deal with Iraq.

September 23, 1990 King Hussein of Jordan publishes his editorial "It's Not Too Late to Prevent a War."

November 1, 1990 More than one million refugees have fled from Iraq and Kuwait since the invasion.

November 8, 1990 Bush announces the deployment of an additional two hundred thousand American troops to the Persian Gulf.

November 29, 1990 The UN Security Council passes Resolution 678, which establishes a deadline of January 15, 1991, for Iraq to withdraw from Kuwait and authorizes members to use force if Iraq fails to comply.

December 6, 1990 Iraq releases remaining Western hostages.

December 24, 1990 Fariba Nawa publishes her essay "A 'Camel Jockey' in an American Classroom" about the treatment of Arabs and Muslims in American society.

January 9, 1991 U.S. Secretary of State James Baker meets with Iraqi Foreign Minister Tariq Aziz in Geneva, Switzerland, but they fail to reach an agreement to avoid war.

January 12, 1991 The U.S. Congress authorizes the president to use force to liberate Kuwait.

January 15, 1991 Iraqi forces fail to withdraw from Kuwait by the UN deadline.

January 16, 1991 President Bush makes a televised speech announcing the start of the Persian Gulf War.

January 17, 1991 A U.S.-led coalition launches an air war against Iraq to begin Operation Desert Storm.

January 18, 1991 Iraq begins firing Scud missiles at Israel.

January 20, 1991 U.S. patriot missiles successfully intercept Iraqi Scud missiles aimed at Dharan, Saudi Arabia.

January 22, 1991 Iraqi soldiers begin setting fire to Kuwait's oil production facilities.

January 23, 1991 U.S. Army General Colin Powell announces that the coalition has achieved air superiority.

January 25, 1991 Iraqi forces release millions of gallons of oil into the Persian Gulf.

January 30, 1991 Iraqi forces capture the Saudi Arabian border town of Khafji.

January 31, 1991 Saudi Arabian troops backed by U.S. Marines reclaim Khafji after an intense battle.

February 13, 1991 U.S. laser-guided bombs destroy a bunker in Baghdad, killing more than one hundred Iraqi civilians.

February 15, 1991 Iraq offers to withdraw from Kuwait but coalition leaders find Iraq's conditions unacceptable and reject the offer.

February 18, 1991 Soviet President Gorbachev announces a new plan to end the war, but Bush rejects it because it does not meet all of the UN Security Council resolutions.

February 22, 1991 Bush sets a deadline of the following day for Iraqi troops to withdraw from Kuwait or face a ground war.

February 24, 1991 The U.S.-led coalition launches a ground war against Iraq.

February 26, 1991 An Iraqi Scud missile hits a U.S. Army camp in Dharan, Saudi Arabia, killing twenty-eight American soldiers.

February 27, 1991 Kuwait City is liberated by coalition forces.

February 28, 1991 Bush declares victory over Iraq and orders a cease-fire.

February 28, 1991 U.S. Army Captain Samuel G. Putnam III describes his experiences during the ground war in a letter to his wife.

March 2, 1991 Shiite Muslims in southern Iraq and Kurds in northern Iraq stage rebellions against Hussein's rule;

Hussein violently crushes the attempts to overthrow his government.

March 3, 1991 Iraq agrees to all allied terms for a permanent cease-fire.

April 3, 1991 The United Nations passes Resolution 687, formally ending the Persian Gulf War.

April 15, 1991 The United Nations conducts the first international weapons inspections in Iraq.

November 1991 The last oil-well fires are extinguished in Kuwait.

1992 The United States establishes a "no-fly zone" in southern Iraq to protect the country's Shiite minority from an attack by the Iraqi air force.

January 1993 Bill Clinton becomes the fortieth president of the United States.

1993 Iraq refuses to cooperate with UN weapons inspectors, and the United States responds by firing cruise missiles at a suspected chemical weapons plant near Baghdad.

1994 Iraq moves troops toward the Kuwait border, but pulls back when the United States sends aircraft carriers to the Persian Gulf.

1995 The UN Security Council Resolution 986 allows Iraq to sell limited amounts of oil in international markets and use the proceeds to buy food.

1995 The Iraqi National Congress launches an unsuccessful coup against Hussein.

1996 Iraqi troops capture Erbil, the capital of the Kurdish-controlled region of northern Iraq. The United States responds by expanding the "no-fly zone" to northern Iraq.

1997 The U.S. House of Representatives launches an investigation into the possible causes of the mysterious collection of ailments among Gulf War veterans known as Gulf War syndrome.

1998 Iraq stops cooperating with UN weapons inspectors, and inspectors leave Iraq.

1998 U.S. and British forces launch Operation Desert Fox, a bombing campaign aimed at destroying suspected weapons of mass destruction in Iraq.

1998 Retired U.S. Air Force fighter pilot Michael Donnelly publishes *Falcon's Cry: A Memoir,* about his experiences in the Persian Gulf War and his struggles with Gulf War syndrome.

January 2001 George W. Bush is inaugurated the forty-first president of the United States.

September 11, 2001 The terrorist group Al Qaeda hijacks four commercial airliners and crashes two into the World Trade Center in New York City, one into the Pentagon near Washington, D.C., and a fourth thwarted attempt into an empty Pennsylvania field, killing more than three thousand people.

January 29, 2002 U.S. President George W. Bush makes his "axis of evil" speech, officially expanding the fight against terrorism to include nations that shelter terrorists or provide weapons, training, or financial support for their activities. Among the countries that he accuses of supporting terrorists are Iraq, Iran, and North Korea.

August 15, 2002 Brent Scowcroft, who served as U.S. national security advisor during the 1991 Persian Gulf War, publishes his editorial "Don't Attack Saddam," expressing his opposition to another war in Iraq.

September 12, 2002 Bush challenges the United Nations to enforce its resolutions against Iraq that ended the 1991 Persian Gulf War.

September 16, 2002 Iraq says it will allow UN inspections to resume "without conditions."

October 11, 2002 The U.S. Congress authorizes the use of military force against Iraq.

November 8, 2002 The UN Security Council passes Resolution 1441, which authorizes a new round of weapons inspections in Iraq and promises "serious consequences" if Hussein fails to comply.

November 18, 2002 Iraq allows UN weapons inspectors to return to the country after a four-year absence.

January 28, 2003 In his second State of the Union address, Bush cites British intelligence reports claiming that

Iraq tried to acquire uranium from Africa to build nuclear weapons.

February 5, 2003 U.S. Secretary of State Colin Powell presents evidence of Iraqi weapons programs to the United Nations.

February 14, 2003 Head UN weapons inspector Hans Blix challenges Powell's evidence and praises Iraq's cooperation with inspections.

February 15, 2003 Large-scale antiwar protests take place in dozens of cities around the world.

February 24, 2003 The United States introduces a new UN resolution authorizing the use of military force to disarm Iraq, but France threatens to veto the resolution.

March 17, 2003 Bush withdraws the proposed UN resolution and gives Hussein and his two sons forty-eight hours to leave Iraq or face a U.S.-led invasion.

March 19, 2003 The United States launches air strikes against targets in Iraq to begin the 2003 Iraq War.

March 20, 2003 U.S. and British ground forces begin advancing into Iraq.

March 21, 2003 Coalition forces launch the "shock and awe" bombing campaign.

March 23, 2003 Members of the U.S. Army's 507th Maintenance Company are ambushed in the city of Nasiriyah.

April 4, 2003 U.S. forces capture Saddam International Airport outside Baghdad.

April 5, 2003 U.S. tanks roll through the streets of Baghdad for the first time.

April 7, 2003 British forces take control of the city of Basra in southern Iraq.

April 9, 2003 A statue of Hussein is toppled in central Baghdad's Firdos Square, symbolizing the fall of the Iraqi regime; looting and violence erupts in the city.

April 14, 2003 The Pentagon declares that major combat operations in Iraq have ended.

April 15, 2003 The first meeting to plan Iraq's future is held in the ancient city of Ur.

May 1, 2003 Bush makes his historic speech aboard the aircraft carrier USS *Abraham Lincoln,* announcing that major combat operations in Iraq are over and that the Iraqi people have been freed from Hussein's rule.

May 12, 2003 American diplomat L. Paul Bremer III arrives in Baghdad to head the Coalition Provisional Authority, the U.S.-led civil administration in charge of Iraq's reconstruction.

May 22, 2003 The UN Security Council passes Resolution 1483, formally recognizing the United States and Great Britain as "occupying powers" in Iraq.

July 6, 2003 Former U.S. Diplomat Joseph Wilson accuses the Bush administration of exaggerating the threat posed by Iraq's alleged weapons programs.

July 13, 2003 The Iraq Governing Council is formed as the first interim government of the new Iraq; it consists of twenty-five prominent Iraqis from diverse ethnic and religious backgrounds.

July 22, 2003 Hussein's two sons, Uday and Qusay, are killed in a firefight with U.S. troops in Mosul.

August 7, 2003 A car bomb explodes outside the Jordanian embassy in Baghdad, marking the first terrorist attack following the fall of Saddam Hussein.

August 19, 2003 A truck bomb explodes outside the UN headquarters in Baghdad, killing twenty-three people, including Sergio Vieira de Mello, the UN Special Representative to Iraq.

August 31, 2003 The number of U.S. troops killed in Iraq following the end of major combat operations surpasses the number killed during the war.

September 7, 2003 Bush asks the U.S. Congress to approve his request for $87 billion to pay for ongoing military and rebuilding efforts in Afghanistan and Iraq.

November 27, 2003 On Thanksgiving, Bush makes a surprise visit to U.S. military forces in Baghdad.

December 13, 2003 Former Iraqi leader Saddam Hussein is captured by U.S. forces.

Words to Know

A

Al Qaeda: A radical Islamic terrorist group responsible for the September 11, 2001, terrorist attacks against the United States.

Annex: To incorporate a country or territory into another country.

Arab League: An alliance of twenty Arab nations and the Palestine Liberation Organization that promotes political, military, and economic cooperation in the Arab world.

Arabs: People of North Africa and the Middle East who speak the Arabic language.

B

Baath Party: A radical political movement founded in the 1940s with the goal of uniting the Arab world and creating one powerful Arab state.

C

Civilians: People not involved in fighting a war, including women and children.

Coalition: A temporary alliance of countries working toward a common goal.

Coalition Provisional Authority: The U.S.-run civil agency in charge of Iraq's 2003 postwar reconstruction.

Cold War: A period of political tension and military rivalry between the United States and the Soviet Union that began in the 1940s and ended with the collapse of the Soviet Union in 1989.

E

Economic sanctions: Trade restrictions intended to punish a country for breaking international law.

F

Fedayeen: A group of Iraqi paramilitary fighters that was intensely loyal to Iraqi President Saddam Hussein.

G

Geneva Conventions: A set of rules developed in Geneva, Switzerland, between 1864 and 1949 that are intended to guarantee the humane treatment of enemy soldiers and prisoners and the protection of civilians during wartime.

I

Insurgency: Organized resistance against an established government or occupying force.

Iran: A non-Arab nation in the Middle East that came under control of Shiite Muslim fundamentalists in 1979 and fought against Iraq during the Iran-Iraq War (1980–88).

Iraq Governing Council (IGC): The first transitional government in Iraq following the 2003 fall of Iraqi President Saddam Hussein; its membership included twenty-five prominent Iraqis whose political, ethnic, and religious backgrounds reflected the diversity of Iraq's population.

Israel: A Middle Eastern state created by the United Nations in 1948 as a homeland for all Jewish people. It is now the scene of major conflicts between the Israeli people and the Palestinians.

K

Kurds: A group of non-Arab Muslim people of northern Iraq who opposed Iraqi President Saddam Hussein's government.

M

Muslims: People who practice the religion of Islam.

O

Organization of Oil Exporting Countries (OPEC): An organization formed in the 1960s by the world's major oil-producing nations to coordinate policies and ensure stable oil prices in world markets.

Ottomans: A group of non-Arab Turkish invaders who conquered much of the Middle East around 1500 and ruled over a vast empire until 1920.

P

Palestine Liberation Organization (PLO): A political organization representing displaced Palestinians. The main goals of the PLO include reclaiming lost territory from Israel and establishing an independent Palestinian state.

Palestinians: An Arab people whose ancestors lived in the region that is now covered by the Jewish state of Israel. The creation of Israel in 1948 displaced hundreds of thousands of Palestinians and contributed to later conflicts in the Middle East.

R

Reconstruction: The process of rebuilding a country's infrastructure, government, and economy following a war.

Republican Guard: An elite, 100,000-man force that was the best-trained and best-equipped part of Iraq's army.

S

Shiite: A branch of the Islamic religion practiced by 15 percent of the world's Muslims, but 60 percent of Iraq's population.

Sunni: A branch of the Islamic religion practiced by 85 percent of the world's Muslims, but only 20 percent of Iraq's population.

T

Taliban: A radical Islamic group that took over the government of Afghanistan in 1996. The Taliban sheltered Osama bin Laden and Al Qaeda, the terrorists behind the attacks against the United States on September 11, 2001.

U

United Nations Security Council: The division of the United Nations charged with maintaining international peace and security. It consists of five permanent member nations (the United States, Russia, Great Britain, France, and China) and ten elected members that serve two-year terms.

People to Know

A

Madeleine Albright (1937–): U.S. ambassador to the United Nations (1993–97) and U.S. secretary of state (1997–2000) under President Bill Clinton.

Tariq Aziz (1936–): Iraqi foreign minister and lead negotiator during the 1991 Persian Gulf War who was captured by coalition forces during the 2003 Iraq War.

B

James Baker (1930–): U.S. secretary of state during the 1991 Persian Gulf War.

Ahmed Hassan al-Bakr (1914–1982): Older cousin of Saddam Hussein and Baath Party leader who served as the president of Iraq from 1968 to 1979.

Osama bin Laden (1957–): Saudi-born Muslim cleric who formed the Al Qaeda terrorist group and organized the September 11, 2001, attacks against the United States.

Tony Blair (1953–): Prime minister of Great Britain during 2003 Iraq War.

L. Paul Bremer III (1941–): American diplomat and head of the Coalition Provisional Authority, the group charged with Iraq's reconstruction.

George H. W. Bush (1924–): President of the United States (1989–93) during the 1991 Persian Gulf War.

George W. Bush (1946–): President of the United States (2001–) during the 2003 Iraq War; son of former president George H. W. Bush.

C

Dick Cheney (1941–): Served as U.S. secretary of defense during the 1991 Persian Gulf War and vice president during the 2003 Iraq War.

Jacques Chirac (1932–): President of France who led international opposition to the 2003 Iraq War.

Bill Clinton (1946–): President of the United States from 1993 to 2001.

Sir Percy Cox (1864–1937): British government official who established the modern borders of Iraq, Saudi Arabia, and Kuwait in 1921.

H

Saddam Hussein (1937–): President of Iraq (1979–2003) during the 1991 Persian Gulf War who was removed from power during the 2003 Iraq War.

K

Ayatollah Khomeini (1900–1989): Islamic religious leader and outspoken opponent of Saddam Hussein who ruled Iran during the Iran-Iraq War (1980–88).

M

Ali Hassan al-Majid (1941–): Iraqi army general known as "Chemical Ali" for allegedly ordering the use of chemical weapons against the Kurdish people of northern Iraq. He was captured following the 2003 Iraq War.

P

Colin Powell (1937–): U.S. military general and chairman of the Joint Chiefs of Staff during the 1991 Persian Gulf War; also served as secretary of state during the 2003 Iraq War.

Q

Abdul Karim Qassem (1914–1963): Military ruler of Iraq from 1958 to 1963, when he was assassinated by members of the Baath Party.

R

Donald Rumsfeld (1932–): U.S. secretary of defense who played a leading role in deciding military strategy for the 2003 Iraq War.

S

Jaber al-Ahmed al-Sabah (1926–): Emir (ruler) of Kuwait during the 1991 Persian Gulf War.

Mohammed Said al-Sahhaf (1940–): Iraqi information minister during the 2003 Iraq War. He became known as "Baghdad Bob" and "Comical Ali" due to his defiant and overly optimistic statements to the media.

H. Norman Schwarzkopf (1934–): U.S. Army general and commander of allied forces during Operation Desert Storm.

T

Margaret Thatcher (1925–): Prime Minister of Great Britain during the 1990 Iraqi invasion of Kuwait.

Saddam Hussein

*Excerpt from a transcript of his July 25, 1990,
meeting with U.S. Ambassador April Glaspie*

Transcript obtained by British journalists on September 2, 1990

On July 25, 1990, a week before Iraq launched its military invasion of Kuwait, Iraqi President Saddam Hussein held a meeting with April Glaspie, the U.S. ambassador to Iraq. This meeting marked the last official high-level contact between the Iraqi and American governments before the invasion. During his meeting with Glaspie, Hussein outlined a long list of complaints against Kuwait. He discussed the ongoing border disputes between the two countries, for example, and also accused Kuwait of pursuing policies that were intended to harm Iraq's economy. Glaspie listened to Hussein's concerns and expressed sympathy for Iraq's financial problems. She also emphasized the U.S. government's wish to maintain friendly relations with Iraq.

The Iraqi government released a transcript (written copy) of the meeting to British journalists on September 2, 1990, a month after Iraq invaded Kuwait. The transcript created a huge controversy when it became public. After reviewing it, some people felt that Hussein had informed Glaspie of his intention to attack Kuwait. They also claimed that Glaspie had led the Iraqi leader to believe that the United

States would not get involved in his dispute with his neighbor. Of course, the United States and most other countries around the world strongly objected to Hussein's invasion of Kuwait and eventually went to war to force Iraq to withdraw.

Disagreements over war debts and oil prices

Many of Hussein's complaints about Kuwait stemmed from the eight-year Iran-Iraq War (1980–88). Hussein argued that he had fought this war against Iran, a non-Arab nation located directly east of Iraq, in order to protect the Arab world from the Islamic fundamentalists (people with extreme beliefs) who had taken over Iran. Kuwait, Saudi Arabia, and many other wealthy Arab nations sided with Iraq and loaned Hussein billions of dollars during the war.

The United States also supported Iraq during the war against Iran. American leaders worried that Iran's religious fundamentalism might spread and increase the turmoil in the Middle East. The United States established diplomatic relations with Iraq in 1984 and began sending shipments of grain and other goods to the country. By 1990 Iraq was America's third-largest trading partner in the Middle East, behind Saudi Arabia and Israel.

The eight-year war against Iran left the Iraqi economy in ruins. Iraq spent an estimated $500 billion to fight the war and owed $80 billion to other countries when it ended. By 1990 Hussein desperately needed money to help his country recover from the effects of the war. He felt that his Arab neighbors should forgive Iraq's debts (not require repayment of loans) since Iraq fought to defend all Arab interests in the Persian Gulf region. Some countries did forgive Iraq's war debts, though Kuwait refused to do so.

Iraq's financial problems grew worse in 1990 because of a steep decline in oil prices. Many countries in the Middle East, including Iraq and Kuwait, contain some of the world's largest underground oil reserves. These countries make money by pumping and exporting oil (selling it to other countries around the world). The Organization of Petroleum Exporting Countries (OPEC) sets limits, or quotas, on the amount of oil its member countries pump each year in order to ensure stable oil prices in world markets. Hussein believed that some OPEC countries, particularly Kuwait and the United Arab Emirates, were involved in a conspiracy to reduce Iraq's power in the Middle East. He argued that they pumped more oil than was allowed under OPEC agreements in a deliberate attempt to lower world oil prices and harm Iraq's economy. He considered these actions by his fellow Arab states to be "economic war" against Iraq.

Finally, Iraq and Kuwait were involved in a longstanding dispute over the border between the two countries and the ownership of off-shore islands in the Persian Gulf. Hussein claimed that Kuwait was trying to expand into Iraqi territory and was stealing oil from underground oil fields on the Iraqi side of the border.

After meeting with U.S. Ambassador April Glaspie, Iraqi President Saddam Hussein incorrectly believed that the United States and other Western powers would not get involved if he invaded Kuwait.
©Reuters NewMedia Inc./Corbis. Reproduced by permission.

Mixed messages and misunderstandings

The time leading up to Iraq's invasion of Kuwait on August 2, 1990, was filled with mixed messages and misunderstandings. Hussein came to believe that the United States and other Western powers would not get involved if he invaded Kuwait. At the same time, world leaders never thought that Hussein would start another war so soon after the conclusion of the damaging and expensive Iran-Iraq War. In an effort to maintain friendly relations with Iraq, these countries overlooked or ignored many signs of Hussein's aggression.

For example, Iraq used chemical weapons during the Iran-Iraq War and afterward against Kurdish rebels in northern Iraq. Western governments also received reports about human-rights abuses in Iraq. These reports claimed that Hussein's government routinely tortured and killed its political opponents. Hussein's regime also used violence and terror to control the media in Iraq. In March 1990, for instance, the Iraqi government executed Farzad Bazoft, a reporter for the *London Observer*. Hussein argued that his government was jus-

Iraq as the "Cradle of Civilization"

Modern-day Iraq covers most of the area that was once known as Mesopotamia. This great ancient civilization developed in the fertile plain between the Tigris and Euphrates rivers between six thousand and seven thousand years ago. The people of Mesopotamia originated many things that have since become fixtures of modern civilization. For example, Mesopotamia was the site of the world's first cities and first legal systems. It saw the earliest use of written language and the earliest practice of organized religion. Mesopotamians were also the first to use wheeled vehicles, to tame livestock, to build canals and dams for irrigation, and to practice the science of astronomy. Such remarkable contributions help explain why Mesopotamia is often referred to as the "cradle of civilization."

The modern nation of Iraq is filled with relics from this ancient civilization. In fact, experts estimate that Iraq contains one hundred thousand sites of historic significance. Only about ten thousand of these sites have been discovered and explored. Many Iraqi cities feature monuments, museums, and other places of cultural or religious importance. For example, the ancient city of Ur in southern Iraq is the biblical birthplace of Abraham, who is considered the father of the world's three major religions (Judaism, Christianity, and Islam). It also contains one of the world's oldest temples, called a ziggurat, dating from 2100 B.C.E. The ancient city of Ninevah in northern Iraq contains palace ruins of Assyrian kings dating back to the seventh century B.C.E. One of these palaces held the first known work of written literature. The city of Samarra, about 100 miles (160.9 kilometers) north of Baghdad, is home to a spectacular mosque with a 150-foot-tall (45.72 meters) spiral minaret (a tower with balconies for calling Muslims to

tified in hanging the foreign journalist because it had evidence that he was a spy. In April 1990 Hussein threatened to use chemical weapons against Israel, which Iraq and many other Arab nations considered to be an enemy.

All of these incidents convinced many people that Hussein was dangerous and unpredictable. He received a great deal of criticism in the international media, and some governments around the world considered using economic sanctions (trade restrictions and other measures designed to hurt another country's economy) to punish him. In the end, however, very little direct action was taken. In fact, U.S. President George H. W. Bush opposed economic sanctions and expressed a desire to expand the friendship between Iraq and prayer) that was constructed in 850 C.E. The major city of Basra is located near where the Tigris and Euphrates rivers meet, a spot that according to legend held the biblical Garden of Eden.

Many historians around the world grew concerned for the safety of these precious sites during the 1991 Persian Gulf War. They worried that bombing campaigns and troop movements in Iraq might lead to massive destruction of ancient artifacts. The United States military employed a team of archaeologists to help them identify historic places so that they would not become targets in the war. But Iraqi leader Saddam Hussein recognized that the American military was trying to protect historic sites from damage, so he sometimes used ancient ruins to hide Iraqi tanks and other military equipment. In addition, many sites were difficult to find and may have suffered accidental destruction.

Following Iraq's defeat in the Persian Gulf War, looters smuggled thousands of priceless artifacts out of the country. Such smuggling continued for the next ten years, as the Iraqi people suffered many hardships under international trade restrictions. Some items regularly appeared on the Internet auction site eBay, while others were sold to private collectors in the huge worldwide market for antiquities.

Sources: Creager, Ellen. "Irreplaceable: Fighting Imperils Priceless Relics of the World's First Civilizations." Detroit Free Press, *April 8, 2003; "Iraq: The Cradle of Civilization at Risk." Available online At http://www2.h-net.msu.edu/~museum/iraq.html (last accessed on April 6, 2004); "Iraq War on Ancient Artifacts of Mesopotamia: What's at Stake in the Iraq War for Lovers of Ancient History." Available online at http://ancienthistory.about.com/library/weekly/ aa031903a.htm (accessed on March 9, 2004); Mazurkewich, Karen. "Ancient Treasures Imperiled in Iraq." Available online at http://www. startribune.com/stories/1375/3794429.html (last accessed on April 6, 2004).*

the United States. He even sent official greetings to Iraq on July 17, 1990, the anniversary of Hussein's rise to power.

It was around this time that Hussein began preparing to invade Kuwait. He made a fiery speech on July 17 in which he accused Kuwait of stealing oil from the Iraqi side of the Rumaila oil field that straddled the border between the two countries. He also began moving Iraqi troops toward the Kuwaiti border. Although U.S. government officials were concerned about these developments, they did not strongly criticize Iraq's actions or directly express their intention to protect Kuwait.

On July 25 Hussein held a meeting with April Glaspie, the U.S. ambassador to Iraq. The Iraqi government released a transcript of this meeting, which is excerpted here.

According to the transcript, Glaspie expresses U.S. concern about the Iraqi troops gathered near the Kuwaiti border. But she also says that the U.S. government has no official position on border disputes in the Middle East and no special defense commitments with Kuwait. Partly on the basis of this conversation, Hussein apparently came to believe that the U.S. government would not send troops to protect Kuwait.

Things to remember while reading the excerpt from the meeting between Saddam Hussein and April Glaspie:

- The transcript of the meeting between Saddam Hussein and April Glaspie was prepared by the Iraqi government. Glaspie claimed that the Iraqis edited her comments in a misleading way in order to make her seem supportive of Hussein's invasion of Kuwait. For example, Glaspie said that the Iraqis had removed strongly worded warnings she issued to Hussein about the American reaction to an invasion of Kuwait. According to Peter Cipkowski in *Understanding the Crisis in the Persian Gulf,* Glaspie later told the U.S. Senate Foreign Relations Committee that she warned Hussein that "we would support our friends in the Gulf, we would defend their sovereignty [independence] and integrity," and that "we would insist on settlements being made in a nonviolent manner, not by threats, not by intimidation, and certainly not by aggression." When the transcript surfaced and created a controversy, according to the *Christian Science Monitor,* Glaspie called it a "fabrication" and expressed "astonishment" that anyone would pay attention to "a document issued by a president whose credibility [honesty] is surely not in high repute [regard]."

- In his meeting with Glaspie, Hussein complains that the American media has launched a negative campaign against him. He is referring to print articles and television reports that focused on his use of chemical weapons and history of human-rights abuses. One example was a report by broadcast journalist Diane Sawyer that aired on the television program "Prime Time Live." It included an interview with Hussein, as well as footage of Kurdish villages in Iraq that had been attacked by the Iraqi army. Glaspie sympathizes with Hussein's complaints about the American media, explaining that they often air critical reports about U.S. political leaders as well. She suggests that he appear on American television to tell his side of the story and help the American people understand his goals.

Excerpt from the transcript of the meeting between Saddam Hussein and April Glaspie

*Saddam Hussein: I have **summoned** you today to hold **comprehensive** political discussions with you. This is a message to President Bush.... Iraq came out of the [Iran-Iraq] war **burdened** with $40 billion **debts**, excluding the aid given by Arab states, some of whom consider that too to be a debt although they know—and you know too—that without Iraq they would not have had these sums and the future of the region would have been entirely different.*

*We began to face the **policy** of the drop in the price of oil. Then we saw the United States, which always talks of democracy but which has no time for the other point of view. Then the media **campaign** against Saddam Hussein was started by the official American media.... We were disturbed by this campaign but we were not disturbed too much because we had hoped that, in a few months, those who are decision makers in America would have a chance to find the facts and see whether this media campaign has had any effect on the lives of Iraqis. We had hoped that soon the American authorities would make the correct decision regarding their relations with Iraq. Those with good relations can sometimes afford to disagree.*

*But when planned and **deliberate** policy forces the price of oil down without good **commercial** reasons, then that means another war against Iraq. Because military war kills people by bleeding them, and **economic war** kills their humanity by **depriving** them of their chance to have a good standard of living. As you know, we gave rivers of blood in a war that lasted eight years, but we did not lose our humanity. Iraqis have a right to live proudly. We do not accept that anyone could injure Iraqi pride or the Iraqi right to have high standards of living.*

Summoned: Called for or demanded.

Comprehensive: All-inclusive or wide-ranging.

Burdened: Loaded down.

Debts: Money owed.

Policy: Plan or course of action.

Campaign: Series of related operations designed to bring about a particular result.

Deliberate: Well thought out.

Commercial: Business-related.

Economic war: Actions intended to harm a nation's economy, or its ability to produce goods and services and care for its citizens.

Depriving: Withholding or taking away from.

*Kuwait and the **U.A.E.** were at the front of this policy aimed at lowering Iraq's position and depriving its people of higher economic standards. And you know that our relations with the Emirates and Kuwait had been good. On top of all that, while we were busy at war, the state of Kuwait began to expand at the expense of our territory.*

*You may say this is **propaganda**, but I would direct you to one document, the Military Patrol Line, which is the borderline endorsed by the **Arab League** in 1961 for military patrols not to cross the Iraq-Kuwait border.*

*But go and look for yourselves. You will see the Kuwaiti border patrols, the Kuwaiti farms, the Kuwaiti oil **installations**—all built as closely as possible to this line to establish that land as Kuwaiti territory....*

We believe that the United States must understand that people who live in luxury and economic security [like Kuwait and the U.A.E.] can reach an understanding with the United States on what are legitimate joint interests. But the starved and the economically deprived [like Iraq] cannot reach the same understanding.

*We do not accept threats from anyone because we do not threaten anyone. But we say clearly that we hope that the U.S. will not entertain too many **illusions** and will seek new friends rather than increase the number of its enemies.*

*I have read the American statements speaking of friends in the area. Of course, it is the right of everyone to choose their friends. We can have no objections. But you know you are not the ones who protected your friends during the war with Iran. I assure you, had the Iranians overrun the region, the American troops would not have stopped them.... So what can it mean when America says it will now protect its friends? It can only mean **prejudice** against Iraq. This stance plus **maneuvers** and statements which have been made has encouraged the U.A.E. and Kuwait to disregard Iraqi rights....*

*We are hurt and upset that such disagreement is taking place between us and Kuwait and the U.A.E. The solution must be found within an Arab framework and through direct **bilateral** relations. We do not place America among the enemies. We place it where we want our friends to be and we try to be friends. But repeated statements last year make it apparent that America did not regard us as friends....*

April Glaspie: Mr. President, you mentioned many things during this meeting which I cannot comment on on behalf of my govern-

U.A.E.: United Arab Emirates, a small Middle Eastern country located southeast of Iraq, near the entrance to the Persian Gulf.

Propaganda: Spreading ideas or information with the intention of helping a certain cause.

Arab League: A political, economic, and military alliance of twenty Arab nations and the Palestine Liberation Organization (PLO).

Installations: Facilities.

Illusions: Mistaken ideas.

Prejudice: Hostile attitudes or negative opinions formed without sufficient knowledge or experience.

Maneuvers: Plans or schemes.

Bilateral: Two-sided.

ment. But with your permission, I will comment on two points. You spoke of friendship and I believe it was clear from the letters sent by our President to you on the occasion of your **National Day** that he emphasizes....

Saddam: He was kind and his expressions met with our regard and respect.

Glaspie: As you know, he directed the United States Administration to reject the suggestion of **implementing** trade **sanctions**.

Saddam: There is nothing left for us to buy from America. Only wheat. Because every time we want to buy something, they say it is forbidden. I am afraid that one day you will say, "You are going to make gunpowder out of wheat."

Glaspie: I have a direct instruction from the President to seek better relations with Iraq....

Saddam: Your stance is generous. We are Arabs. It is enough for us that someone says, "I am sorry, I made a mistake." Then we carry on. But the media campaign continued. And it is full of stories. If the stories were true, no one would get upset. But we understand from its continuation that there is a **determination**.

Glaspie: I saw the **Diane Sawyer** program ["Prime Time Live"] on **ABC**. And what happened in that program was cheap and unjust. And this is a real picture of what happens in the American media—even to American politicians themselves. These are the methods the **Western** media employs. I am pleased that you add your voice to the **diplomats** who stand up to the media. Because your appearance in the media, even for five minutes, would help us to make the American people understand Iraq. This would increase **mutual** understanding. If the American President had control of the media, his job would be much better.

Mr. President, not only do I want to say that President Bush wanted better and deeper relations with Iraq, but he also wants an Iraqi contribution to peace and **prosperity** in the Middle East. President Bush is an intelligent man. He is not going to declare an economic war against Iraq.... I admire your extraordinary efforts to rebuild your country. I know you need funds. We understand that and our opinion is that you should have the opportunity to rebuild your country. But we have no opinion on the Arab-Arab conflicts, like your border disagreement with Kuwait....

Frankly, we can only see that you have **deployed** massive troops in the south. Normally that would not be any of our business. But

National Day: July 17, an Iraqi holiday recognizing the date in 1979 that Saddam Hussein became president.

Implementing: Establishing or putting in place.

Sanctions: Trade restrictions designed to punish a country for breaking international law by harming its economy; in this case, the sanctions were proposed to punish Iraq for human-rights abuses.

Determination: A firm or definite decision.

Diane Sawyer: An American broadcast journalist who interviewed Saddam Hussein and presented a special report on human-rights abuses in Iraq under his government.

ABC: American Broadcasting Company, a U.S. television network.

Western: The noncommunist countries of Western Europe and North America.

Diplomats: Officials that are skilled in negotiation.

Mutual: Joint or shared.

Prosperity: Wealth or well-being.

Deployed: Moved into battle formation.

when this happens in the context of what you said on your National Day, then when we read the details in the two letters of the **Foreign Minister**, then when we see the Iraqi point of view that the **measure** taken by the U.A.E. and Kuwait is, in the final analysis, **parallel** to military aggression against Iraq, then it would be reasonable for me to be concerned. And for this reason, I received an instruction to ask you, in the spirit of friendship—not in the spirit of **confrontation**—regarding your intentions.

I simply describe the concern of my government. And I do not mean that the situation is a simple situation. But our concern is a simple one.

Saddam: We do not ask people not to be concerned when peace is at issue. This is a noble human feeling which we all feel. It is natural for you as a superpower to be concerned. But what we ask is not to express your concern in a way that would make an aggressor believe that he is getting support for his aggression. We want to find a solution which will give us our rights but not deprive others of their rights. But at the same time, we want the others to know that our patience is running out regarding their action.... I told the Arab Kings and Presidents that some brothers are fighting an economic war against us. And that not all wars use weapons and we regard this kind of war as a military action against us.... Before this, I had sent them **envoys** reminding them that our war had included their defense. Therefore the aid they gave us should not be regarded as a debt. We did not more than the United States would have done against someone who attacked its interests....

Glaspie: Mr. President, it would be helpful if you could give us an **assessment** of the effort [at finding a peaceful resolution of the situation] made by your Arab brothers and whether they have achieved anything.

Saddam: [Iraqi and Kuwaiti officials have agreed to meet in Saudi Arabia, in the presence of Saudi officials and President Hosni Mubarak of Egypt.] Then the meeting will be transferred to Baghdad for deeper discussion between Kuwait and Iraq. We hope we will reach some result. We hope that the long-term view and the real interests will overcome Kuwaiti greed.... Brother President Mubarak told me [the Kuwaitis] were scared. They said troops were only 20 kilometers north of the Arab League line. I said to him that regardless of what is there, whether they are police, border guards, or army, and regardless of how many are there, and what they are doing, assure the Kuwaitis and give them our word that we are not

Foreign Minister: Iraqi Foreign Minister Tariq Aziz, who was present at this meeting.

Measure: Action.

Parallel: Similar.

Confrontation: Argument or conflict.

Envoys: Official messengers or representatives.

Assessment: Estimate or opinion.

going to do anything until we meet with them. When we meet and when we see that there is hope, then nothing will happen. But if we are unable to find a solution, then it will be natural that Iraq will not accept death, even though wisdom is above everything else. There you have the good news.

[The conversation concludes when Glaspie agrees to return to Washington, D.C., and deliver Saddam Hussein's message to President Bush.]

What happened next...

A few days after the meeting between Saddam Hussein and U.S. Ambassador April Glaspie, high-ranking Iraqi and Kuwaiti officials met in Jedda, Saudi Arabia. During these talks, Iraq threatened to proceed with an invasion of Kuwait unless the Kuwaiti government met a series of demands.

Iraq demanded that Kuwait forgive its war debts, limit future oil production, and give Iraq control over the disputed island of Bubiyan in the Persian Gulf. Kuwaiti leaders agreed to limit their country's production of oil, and they also expressed a willingness to continue discussing Iraq's other concerns. In the meantime, however, Hussein continued sending troops to the Kuwaiti border. On August 2, 1990, to the shock of many people in the Middle East and around the world, Iraq announced the postponement of future peace talks and launched its invasion of Kuwait.

A month later, British journalists obtained the Iraqi transcript of the meeting between Hussein and Glaspie. It created a major controversy, as people around the world accused Glaspie of encouraging Iraq's aggression. In April 1991, following the U.S.-led coalition's victory in the Persian Gulf War, Glaspie was asked to testify before the U.S. Senate Foreign Relations Committee. She answered a series of questions about her meeting with Hussein. She told the committee members that the transcript did not reflect the true nature of her comments, and claimed that she was the victim of "deliberate deception" by the Iraqi government. In 1992

April Glaspie, U.S. ambassador to Iraq, claimed that the transcript of her meeting with Saddam Hussein that was released did not reflect the true nature of her comments. She also claimed that she was the victim of "deliberate deception" by the Iraqi government. ©Reuters NewMedia Inc./Corbis. Reproduced by permission.

her claims received some support from Iraqi Foreign Minister Tariq Aziz, who had been present at the meeting between Hussein and Glaspie. According to the *Christian Science Monitor*, Aziz said that Glaspie "just listened and made general comments. We knew the United States would have a strong reaction [to Iraq's invasion of Kuwait]."

Did you know...

• April Glaspie was the first woman ever to serve as U.S. ambassador to an Arab country.

• This famous meeting marked the first time Glaspie had ever spoken directly with Saddam Hussein during her three years of service as the U.S. ambassador to Iraq. She only learned that she would be meeting with the Iraqi president a few minutes before being taken into his office.

• At the time Iraq invaded Kuwait, the United States imported 52 percent of its oil, the highest percentage to that point in U.S. history. More than 11 percent of this total came from the Persian Gulf region. Some people argued that America's dependence on foreign oil helped explain why the U.S. government tried so hard to maintain friendly relations with Hussein, as well as why it eventually went to war to liberate Kuwait.

For More Information

Cipkowski, Peter. *Understanding the Crisis in the Persian Gulf.* New York: John Wiley, 1992.

Cole, Carlton. "Whatever Happened to U.S. Ambassador April Glaspie?" *Christian Science Monitor,* May 27, 1999. Available online at http://csmweb2.emcweb.com/durable/1999/05/27/p23s3.htm (accessed on March 2, 2004).

"Excerpts from Iraqi Document on Meeting with U.S. Envoy." *New York Times International,* September 23, 1990. Available online at http://www.chss.montclair.edu/english/furr/glaspie.html (accessed on March 2, 2004).

King, John. *The Gulf War.* New York: Dillon Press, 1991.

Ridgeway, James, ed. *The March to War.* New York: Four Walls Eight Windows, 1991.

Hussein ibn Talal, King of Jordan

Excerpt from his editorial "It's Not Too Late to Prevent a War"

Published in the *Washington Post*, September 23, 1990

During the months between Iraq's invasion of Kuwait in August 1990 and the start of the Persian Gulf War in January 1991, King Hussein of Jordan emerged as one of main figures behind efforts to negotiate a peaceful resolution to the crisis. King Hussein (no relation to Iraqi leader Saddam Hussein) had long maintained friendly relations with both Iraq and the United States.

King Hussein initially declared that Jordan would remain neutral in the conflict and tried to act as a mediator between the two sides. He stressed the importance of Arab participation in solving the problems in the Middle East, and he traveled widely in the Arab world to try to build support for a diplomatic solution. But the king faced a great deal of pressure from within his own country. The majority of Jordanians sympathized with Iraq's position, and King Hussein found that he could not disregard their feelings without risking his hold on power. As a result, Jordan ended up supporting Iraq during the Persian Gulf War.

Jordan and the Palestinians

Jordan is a central state in the Middle East. It is surrounded by Syria to the north, Iraq to the east, Saudi Arabia to the south, and Israel to the west. Half of Jordan's population of 5.5 million are Palestinians. The Palestinians are an Arab people whose ancestors have lived in the Middle East since ancient times. They once made their home in a region known as Palestine, located between the Jordan River and the Mediterranean Sea. Today, the Jewish state of Israel covers most of this territory, which Jews also regard as their historic holy land.

Israel was created by the United Nations in 1948 as a homeland for all Jewish people. When Israel became a Jewish state, hundreds of thousands of Palestinians fled. Since control of their traditional territory had been turned over to people they had long considered rivals, they worried that they would be denied basic rights in Israel. Many Palestinians became refugees in Jordan and other neighboring countries. Some of the displaced Palestinians formed a group called the Palestine Liberation Organization (PLO). The purpose of the PLO was to fight to reclaim lost territory and establish an independent Palestinian state. The PLO often resorted to acts of violence and terrorism in its dispute against Israel. It gained the support of many Arab nations, however, and was eventually recognized by the United Nations as the legitimate government of Palestine. Given the large number of Palestinians who reside in Jordan, the issue of Palestinian statehood is a very important part of Jordan's government policies.

King Hussein takes the throne

Hussein ibn Talal became the king of Jordan in 1952, just a few years after the creation of Israel sent Palestinian refugees streaming into his country. Although he was only seventeen years old at that time, he had spent his life preparing to ascend to the throne. He was raised in a politically powerful family. His grandfather, Abdullah, became the first ruler of the modern state of Jordan after it was created in 1921. King Abdullah led the country until 1951, when he was assassinated by a Palestinian extremist (a person who is radical in his or her beliefs).

Upon taking the throne, King Hussein proved to be a moderate leader whose policies tended to favor the West (the noncommunist countries of Western Europe and North America). His political views brought him into conflict with some other Arab leaders, however, as well as with Jordan's large Palestinian population. Some people viewed him as a pawn of the United States and other Western powers. In fact, he survived a dozen assassination attempts during the early years of his rule.

Despite King Hussein's moderate views, Jordan joined its neighbors Syria and Egypt in a war against Israel in 1967. Known as the Arab-Israeli War or the Six-Day War, this conflict quickly ended in a victory for Israel. As a result of the fighting, the Jewish state took control over an area of Jordan located on the west side of the Jordan River, known as the West Bank, which had once been part of ancient Palestine. This 3,726-square-mile (6,000-square-kilometer) area contained half of Jordan's population as well as a large portion of its industrial base. It also contained a number of important religious sites for Jews, Christians, and Muslims.

During the months before the Persian Gulf War, King Hussein of Jordan worked to negotiate a peaceful resolution to the crisis. *Photograph by Dirck Halstead. Time Life Pictures/Getty Images. Reproduced by permission.*

The loss of the West Bank angered Jordan's Palestinian population. Palestinian extremists stepped up their efforts to overthrow the king, which resulted in a civil war in Jordan in 1970. But King Hussein maintained control of the national army and held the loyalty of many citizens. He eventually was able to win the war and strengthen his rule. In 1974 the king made an agreement with the PLO that helped ease tensions with the Palestinians in his country. Jordan gave up its claims on the West Bank, which remained under occupation by the Israeli army, and recognized the Palestinians as the rightful owners of the disputed territory.

King Hussein's popularity grew, and by the 1980s he was the longest-ruling head of state in the world. He also became a leading figure in Middle Eastern affairs. Jordan supported Iraq during its eight-year war with Iran (1980–88). During this conflict, King Hussein developed a friendship with Saddam Hussein and came to regard the Iraqi leader as a dedicated fighter for Arab causes.

The king's dilemma

When Iraq invaded Kuwait in 1990, King Hussein found himself in a difficult position. As a head of state, he understood that one country should not be allowed simply to overrun another. He respected Kuwait's status as a sovereign nation and spoke out against Iraq's aggression toward its neighbor. Many other Arab leaders felt the same way. In fact, several Arab nations joined the U.S.-led coalition against Iraq.

On the other hand, the PLO openly expressed its support for Saddam and his invasion of Kuwait. Palestinian leaders viewed Saddam as a powerful opponent of Israel and the United States. They also appreciated the fact that Saddam supported the PLO in its fight to establish an independent Palestinian state. King Hussein recognized that Jordan's large Palestinian population would likely follow the PLO's lead and support Iraq. In fact, polls showed that 70 percent of Jordanians approved of Saddam's actions. The king felt that he could not ignore the feelings of the majority of his people. He worried that turning against Iraq would cause huge protests in Jordan and put his rule at risk.

Immediately after Iraq invaded Kuwait, King Hussein declared that Jordan would remain neutral (not take sides) in the conflict. Over the next few months, he traveled widely in the Arab world to meet with other heads of state. The king tried to use his influence in the region to negotiate a peaceful solution to the crisis. He also met with Saddam to try to convince him to withdraw from Kuwait. King Hussein desperately wanted to avoid a war, which he felt would have harmful effects throughout the Arab world. In the following excerpt from his editorial titled "It's Not Too Late to Prevent a War," published in the *Washington Post* in September 1990, he takes his case to the American people.

Things to remember while reading the excerpt from "It's Not Too Late to Prevent a War" by King Hussein of Jordan:

- In his editorial, King Hussein compares the situation in the Middle East in 1990 to events that took place in August 1914. He is referring to the beginning of World War I (1914–18), in which the Allied Powers (chiefly France, Great Britain, Russia, and the United States) defeated the Central Powers (led by Germany, Austria-Hungary, and Turkey). Following a series of disagreements and conflicts, all of the major countries involved declared war on one another in August 1914. The four years of bloody fighting that followed took the lives of ten million people worldwide. In using this reference, King Hussein is expressing his concern that a war against Iraq could expand into a world war.

- King Hussein also mentions the concept of creating a "new world order." American leaders first began discussing this concept at the end of the Cold War. The Cold War was not an actual war, but a period of political tension and military rivalry between the United States and the Soviet Union (along with their allies) that began in the late 1940s, following the end of World War II (1939–45). During this period, U.S. foreign policy focused on preventing the Communist form of government practiced in the Soviet Union from spreading around the world. (Communism is a political theory in which the government controls the means of production.) When the Soviet Union collapsed in 1989, many other communist governments collapsed as well. U.S. leaders saw the end of the Cold War as a great opportunity to help create new democratic governments around the world, thus establishing a "new world order."

Excerpt from
"It's Not Too Late to Prevent a War"

*Is it too late to prevent another major war in the Middle East? Is the pace of events **accelerating** at such an uncontrollable rate*

Accelerating: Speeding up.

Inevitable: Impossible to prevent.

Conflagration: Burning conflict.

Spoils: Rewards of victory.

Embarked: Starting out.

Abolition: Complete destruction.

Quixotic: Foolish or rash.

Concede: Accept or acknowledge.

Conceive: Understand or imagine.

Disputants: Parties to an argument.

Conciliation: Compromise; finding areas of agreement.

Distributive: Provided fairly to all groups.

Selective: Provided only to certain groups.

Inexcusable: Impossible to excuse or justify.

Imposition: Established or put in place.

Marshaling: Organizing.

Sanctions: Trade restrictions used to penalize a country by harming its economy.

Colossal: Huge.

Confines: Borders.

Reverberate: Continue to be felt.

Imperative: Necessary; cannot be avoided.

Vacuum: Isolation; in the absence of outside influences.

Sequentially: Step by step.

*that war is **inevitable**? Are the opposing parties so locked into their positions that a peaceful solution is no longer possible?*

*It is the sad conclusion of many of those who live in the area, and who would be the innocent victims of such a **conflagration**, that the answer is probably yes. And it is part of their despair that they are helpless to do anything about it.*

*One might ask how such a tragic turn of events could have occurred in the space of less than two months. Would there be any victors, and what would be the **spoils**? Are we **embarked** on a noble mission to establish a new world order of peace and justice and the **abolition** of aggression? Or are we witnessing a replay of the **quixotic** events of August 1914, when the world stumbled into a war it did not want but could not stop?*

*I am stubborn enough to believe there is still a chance to prevent another war. I refuse to **concede** that the pace of events cannot be brought under control. And I cannot **conceive** that **disputants** would commit themselves to a war that is so obviously contrary to their own vital interests.*

As for victors and spoils, Middle East wars have produced neither, only graveyards for illusions and the seeds for future wars.

*Let us hope that a new world order can be established, but its foundation must be based on **conciliation**, not conflagration, and on **distributive**, not **selective** justice and morality.*

*I fear the current course of events in the Middle East could, indeed, be a replay of August 1914. To repeat the scenario would be an **inexcusable** tragedy. If the same effort by the world community in the present **marshaling** of military forces, the **imposition** of **sanctions**, and the commitment of **colossal** sums of money were to be applied to a political solution, I am convinced it could be achieved.*

*It is very disturbing that some believe military action is the only solution to the current crisis. This is dangerously short-sighted. The effects of a war against Iraq would not be limited to the **confines** of that country. They would **reverberate** in every capital throughout the Middle East. They would create the very instability such action was designed to prevent. For these reasons a political solution to the present crisis is **imperative**.*

*Since the Iraqi invasion of Kuwait did not occur in a **vacuum**, it cannot be solved in a vacuum. Any solution must address, if not simultaneously at least **sequentially**, the major underlying causes—*

*namely, the dispute between Iraq and Kuwait, the confrontation between Israel, Palestine, and the Arab States, and the **perilous escalation** and **proliferation** of weapons of mass destruction.*

*All of these problems are driven by political differences. To attempt to solve them militarily treats only the symptoms, not the causes, and can only **exacerbate** the problems, not resolve them.*

Because these problems are inter-related, piecemeal solutions are not the answer, as efforts over several years have demonstrated.

*This is not as tall an order as it sounds, since proposed solutions to some of these problems already exist in the files of those governments involved. The area is exhausted from the conflicts and tensions it has endured for decades. Most are **appalled** by the wasteful **diversion** of so much wealth and energy to the misfortunes of war. They are eager to join the rest of the world in its new march toward freedom, justice, and prosperity. Despite the threat of war, the conditions for peace do exist in the Middle East. It is a moment of opportunity, which we should all grasp.*

*Whatever political solution to the immediate crisis might be devised, I believe it imperative that it include a substantial Arab input. **Irrespective** of the justice of any solution, there must not be room to misrepresent it as a resolution imposed from outside the area. This would only **discredit** its legitimacy.*

*Finally, there is one thing of which I am certain. The Middle East cannot afford another war. The world should not impose one on it. I am also certain that it is not beyond the **ingenuity** of the leaders of this world to devise a peaceful solution to this crisis. May God help us all if they cannot.*

Perilous: Dangerous.

Escalation: Increase in number or scale.

Proliferation: Spreading or growth.

Exacerbate: Complicate or make worse.

Appalled: Shocked or horrified.

Diversion: Redirect or change course.

Irrespective: Without regard to.

Discredit: Cast doubt on.

Ingenuity: Cleverness or skill.

What happened next...

As time passed and war in the Persian Gulf became increasingly likely, King Hussein gradually shifted his support toward Iraq. When other Arab nations joined the U.S.-led coalition against Iraq in the fall of 1990, Jordan refused to do so. In fact, Jordan continued to trade with Iraq illegally after the United Nations imposed economic sanctions (strict re-

As the start of the war loomed closer, hundreds of thousands of refugees from countries in the Persian Gulf region flooded into Jordan for safety. ©Francoise de Mulder/Corbis. Reproduced by permission.

strictions on trade that are intended to punish a country for breaking international law) against Saddam.

When the Persian Gulf War began in January 1991, Jordan provided some limited military assistance to Iraq. In addition, Iraqi Scud missiles (Soviet-made missiles with limited range and accuracy) flew through Jordanian air space on their way to hit targets in Israel. King Hussein's support of Iraq led to strained relations between Jordan and the countries that joined the coalition. Many of these countries stopped trading with Jordan and cut off international aid payments. As a result, Jordan's economy struggled and its people suffered many hardships during the war.

Once the war ended, however, King Hussein worked to improve Jordan's economy and also gave his people greater freedoms. His actions helped Jordan regain the favor of its Arab neighbors, as well as Western powers. King Hussein went on to play a leading role in peace negotiations between the

Arabs and Israelis. In 1994 Jordan signed a peace treaty with Israel. By the time he died of cancer in 1999, King Hussein was highly regarded throughout the world as a peacemaker. He was succeeded on the throne by his son Abdullah II.

Did you know...

- When King Hussein wrote his editorial, Jordan was struggling to meet the needs of hundreds of thousands of refugees. People began crossing into Jordan from Iraq and Kuwait shortly after Saddam launched his invasion. As war loomed closer, more people from these countries and others in the Persian Gulf region joined the flow of refugees into Jordan. Throughout the course of the Persian Gulf War, seven hundred fifty thousand refugees made their way into Jordan, putting stress on King Hussein's government and the Jordanian people. International relief agencies like the Red Cross sent shipments of food, medicine, clothing, and shelter to help the refugees. Once the war began, however, King Hussein received very little aid from Western nations or the Arab countries that had joined the coalition against Iraq.

- At the time of his death in 1999, King Hussein was married to his fourth wife, Queen Noor. She was an American citizen who was known as Lisa Halaby before she married into Jordan's royal family. They had two sons and two daughters together. King Hussein also had seven other children from his three previous marriages.

- As the United States appeared likely to go to war against Iraq for a second time in early 2003, Jordan seemed willing to switch sides. The U.S. and Jordanian governments negotiated an arrangement that would allow American warplanes to fly combat missions over Jordan's air space. The two countries also discussed the possibility of stationing some U.S. troops in Jordan or placing Patriot missile batteries within Jordan in order to shoot down Iraqi missiles aimed at Israel.

For More Information

Cipkowski, Peter. *Understanding the Crisis in the Persian Gulf.* New York: Wiley, 1992.

"Hussein I, King of Jordan." *Current Leaders of Nations,* 1998. Reproduced in *Biography Resource Center.* Farmington Hills, MI: Gale Group, 2003.

"Hussein ibn Talal." *Encyclopedia of World Biography,* 2nd ed., 1998. Reproduced in *Biography Resource Center.* Farmington Hills, MI: Gale Group, 2003.

Ridgeway, James, ed. *The March to War.* New York: Four Walls Eight Windows, 1991.

Fariba Nawa

Excerpt from her essay "A 'Camel Jockey' in an American Classroom"

Published by the Pacific News Service, December 24, 1990

When Iraqi leader Saddam Hussein ordered his military to invade Kuwait in August 1990, he set in motion a series of events that led to the Persian Gulf War. In November 1990 the United Nations Security Council set a deadline of January 15, 1991, for Iraq to withdraw from Kuwait. As this deadline grew closer, the people of the United States began to prepare themselves for war.

Many Americans felt angry and frustrated about the events that were taking place in the Middle East. They worried about the possibility of a long and costly war and about the welfare of U.S. military troops in the Persian Gulf. Unfortunately, these concerns led some Americans to blame all Arabs and Muslims for the actions of Saddam Hussein.

Before the United States became involved in the Persian Gulf War, the country's Arab and Muslim residents largely went unnoticed. Yet the United States was home to more than eight hundred seventy thousand people of Arab ancestry, as well as a large and growing Muslim population. An estimated one billion people around the world practiced the religion of Islam, including five million in the United States.

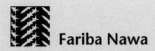

Fariba Nawa

Fariba Nawa was born in Herat, Afghanistan, in 1973. She was six years old when the Soviet Union launched its invasion of Afghanistan. The Soviets installed a Communist government in Afghanistan and used their military strength to keep this government in power. Various Afghan rebel groups, some of which received weapons and financial support from the United States, fought a bitter war against the Soviet troops. During this fighting a bomb destroyed Nawa's elementary school and killed some of her classmates. This incident convinced her family to leave the country in 1981.

Nawa's family walked across the desert for six hours, with donkeys carrying their belongings, until they reached the border of Iran. They waited in a refugee camp there for ten months before they finally received permission to enter the United States in 1982. They settled in California, in one of the largest communities of Afghan exiles in the country. Nawa, who was nine years old at this time, attended public schools in Union City, California. She quickly learned to speak English and became Americanized in appearance.

Throughout her school years, Nawa enjoyed writing and always followed current events. She dreamed of becoming a foreign correspondent for a major news agency someday. In late 1990, a few weeks before the start of the Persian Gulf War, the teenaged Nawa wrote an essay describing her feelings about being a Muslim in American society. This essay, titled "A 'Camel Jockey' in an American Classroom," was published by the Pacific News Service and helped launch her career in journalism.

Among American Muslims, around 33 percent traced their ethnic origin to South Asia (India, Pakistan, and Afghanistan), 30 percent to Africa, and 25 percent to Arab nations. Several U.S. states contained sizeable Muslim communities, with the largest found in California and New York.

In the weeks leading up to the Persian Gulf War, some Arab Americans and Muslim Americans were mistreated, and in some cases threatened or attacked, by other Americans. Some people called for the deportation (forced removal) of all Arabs and Muslims from the United States. Other people vandalized mosques (Muslim places of worship) or Arab-owned businesses. In her essay titled "A 'Camel Jockey' in an American Classroom," a Muslim teenager named Fariba Nawa observes that such hateful attitudes could even be found in the nation's schools.

Nawa earned a bachelor's degree from Hampshire College in Amherst, Massachusetts, in 1996. She then worked as a reporter for a local newspaper in California for two years to gain experience. Part of her job involved covering the Afghan refugee community in Fremont, California. She later continued her education at New York University, where she pursued a graduate degree in Middle Eastern studies and journalism. She also worked as a free-lance journalist for the *Pacific News Service, San Francisco Chronicle, Village Voice,* and *Mother Jones.*

In 2000 Nawa returned to Afghanistan for the first time in eighteen years. She found that the Afghan people enjoyed more freedom than she expected under Taliban rule, although many of their rules were harsh. In 2001 Nawa traveled to Pakistan, where she worked with Afghan refugees who had fled the American bombing that took place in retaliation for the terrorist attacks of September 11. She hoped to return to Afghanistan to report on the effects of the war and efforts to rebuild her home country. Nawa also encouraged other Afghanis living in the West to find a way to help. "It's essential that we do not surrender and leave our Afghanistan a drug-infested haven for terrorism and war," she stated in her essay "Half Way Home."

Sources: Nawa, Fariba. "Half Way Home." Lemar-Aftaab, *July–December 2000. Available online at http://www.afghanmagazine.com/july2000/essays/fariba/index.html (accessed on March 2, 2004); Nawa, Fariba. "Home after 20 Years: Travel to Herat."* Lemar-Aftaab, *January–December 2001. Available online at http://www.afghanmagazine.com/2001/travelogue/faribatravelogue/ (accessed on March 2, 2004).*

Things to remember while reading the excerpt from Fariba Nawa's essay "A 'Camel Jockey' in an American Classroom":

- Nawa arrived in the United States as a refugee from Afghanistan, a country of South Asia located east of Iran and northwest of Pakistan. Afghanistan is one of the poorest countries in the world and has struggled with political instability and violence for many years. In 1979 the Soviet Union made the decision to send troops into Afghanistan and install a Communist government. (Communism is a form of government where one party holds the means of production and distribution of goods.) But the country's many ethnic groups formed rebel armies and fought a bitter war against the Soviet troops. The Soviet Union finally withdrew from Afghanistan in 1989, leaving the various factions to fight for control of the country. In 1996 a radical Islamic group called the Taliban took over the government and imposed strict laws on the Afghani people. "In the name of religion, they forbid women from going to school or working in most fields and force men to pray," Nawa explained in a 2001 essay titled "Home after Twenty Years." "Women must travel with a male kin and wear a burqa, which covers the body like a tent with only a mesh for sight." Some Afghan women were stoned to death for disobeying the Taliban's laws. Huge numbers of refugees fled from Afghanistan following the Soviet invasion, during the later civil wars, and when the Taliban came to power. An estimated 2.5 million Afghanis escaped to Pakistan and 1.5 million to Iran. About one hundred fifty thousand made it to the United States or Western Europe.

- In her essay Nawa mentions that Japanese Americans were treated badly by the U.S. government during World War II (1939–45). On December 7, 1941, Japanese warplanes attacked a U.S. military base in Pearl Harbor, Hawaii. The United States then declared war on Japan and entered World War II. The attack on Pearl Harbor left many Americans angry and frightened. Some people focused their anger on the thousands of people of Japanese descent who lived in the United States. The U.S. government also began to view Japanese Americans with suspicion, worrying that they might engage in spying or sabotage to help Japan's war effort. Over the next few weeks, government agents arrested many leaders of the Japanese immigrant community whom they suspected of disloyalty. In early 1942 President Franklin D. Roosevelt signed Executive Order 9066, which allowed the forced removal of Japanese Americans from sensitive military areas. The U.S. government used this order to remove one hundred twelve thousand people of Japanese descent, about two-thirds of whom were American citizens, from coastal Washington, Oregon, and California. These people were relocated to internment camps in the nation's interior. They lived in military-style barracks and suffered many hardships for the duration of the war. Many Japanese Americans lost their homes, property, and jobs during this time. Years later the U.S. government issued an offi-

cial apology for violating the civil rights of Japanese Americans during World War II. In 1990 the government paid $20,000 in reparations (money paid to people that were wronged by a government) to each surviving Japanese internee. Nawa refers to this ugly chapter of American history because she is concerned that Muslim Americans might be treated similarly during the Persian Gulf War.

• Nawa recalls that one of her teachers led a class discussion about the treatment of women in Saudi Arabia. Saudi Arabia is an Arab country in the Middle East that was part of the coalition against Iraq during the Persian Gulf War. The Saudi government established rules to guide the behavior of its citizens based on Islamic law and Arabic customs. Some of these rules restricted the activities of women. For example, women in Saudi Arabia were not allowed to drive cars and were required to walk twelve paces, or steps, behind men. They were also expected to dress modestly at

In her essay titled "A 'Camel Jockey' in an American Classroom," Fariba Nawa expressed concern that Muslim Americans, including students like the ones pictured here, would be mistreated by other Americans during the Persian Gulf War.
Photograph by Millard Berry. Reproduced by permission.

all times, which meant keeping their hair, arms, and legs covered in public and not wearing bright colors. In her essay Nawa points out that such restrictions did not exist in many other Arab and Muslim countries.

Excerpt from
"A 'Camel Jockey' in an American Classroom"

*With my blond hair and American accent no one would guess I'm an **Afghan-born**, Muslim-raised teenager. In school, I blend in with the crowd. At home, however, my mother still wears a scarf and reads the **Koran**.*

Since the Gulf crisis began, I've felt an increased tension between Muslim students and the rest of the kids in my suburban California high school—a kind of Muslim bashing. "Why do Muslims want to be terrorists?" people ask in classes.

*My classmates don't apply the **stereotypes** they have of Muslims and Arabs to me, but I'm reminded of them constantly. They make jokes about my religion. I've heard them call Muslims names like "maddas lovers," referring to **Saddam**'s name spelled backwards. It makes Muslims seem even more demon-like.*

*They confuse Islam with **Hinduism.** When they find out I'm a Muslim, they ask: "Do you worship cows?"; "Don't you wear red dots on your foreheads?" One boy even asked if Muslims were born with those dots.*

From the day I came to the United States as a refugee at the age of 10 in 1983, I don't remember once learning about Islam at school although I've studied both Christianity and some Judaism. My "World Studies" textbooks in the seventh and ninth grades had small sections about Islam, but the teachers never got around to teaching them.

*In a recent history class my teacher talked about the way Muslims treat their women. He sounded disapproving. As an example of how **repressive** Islam was he pointed out that the Saudis don't allow women to drive and asked what the class thought of that. There was a lot of snickering. Some students cracked jokes about how stupid the Saudis and Muslims must be. The teacher gave us*

Afghan-born: Born in Afghanistan, a country of South Asia located east of Iran and northwest of Pakistan.

Koran: The holy book of the Islamic religion.

Stereotypes: False or oversimplified ideas about the characteristics of a group of people.

Saddam: Iraqi leader Saddam Hussein.

Hinduism: A religious and cultural movement based in India.

Repressive: Exerting strict control over people's lives and denying their basic freedoms.

*no broader information about Islamic culture or the particular **interpretation** of the Koran followed by the Saudis.*

While women can't drive in Saudi Arabia, next door in Kuwait, before the Iraqi invasion, 60 percent of university professors were female. In Iraq, 40 percent of the civil service is made up of women.

I finally stood up and told the class I was a Muslim, that I soon hope to have a driver's license, and that the Koran teaches that men and women are equal. Then I asked how Americans can condemn and judge Muslims without knowing anything about the culture or the religion.

*Islam is practiced widely, from Nigeria to the Philippines. Each culture interprets Islam in a different way, creating their own rules of dress, prayer, and **morality**. Islam is a religion with one billion **adherents** worldwide; it is also the fastest-growing religion in the U.S.— soon to be the second-largest domestically, behind Christianity.*

*How will my classmates deal with a world that is one-quarter Muslim when they do not learn anything about it in school? Many of their parents already have strong **prejudices** against it. I find the same slurs and jokes out of school, written on bumper stickers, in editorial cartoons, and on the radio—names like "camel jockey."*

*Muslims often stay to themselves and in that way stick out more than other cultural minorities. If people's husbands and children start dying in the Persian Gulf, they will make an easy **scapegoat**. Japanese Americans were **ostracized** in World War II, and sometimes I fear the same thing could happen to American Muslims in a Gulf war. The bottom line is that we need better education about Islam and the Middle East. Yet even though Islam is getting some attention because of what's happening in the Gulf, most of it is negative. My only hope is that at least in the schools students will start learning that Islam and Saddam Hussein are not identical. Education in the end is the only force that can break through stereotypes.*

Interpretation: Understanding or explanation.

Morality: Codes of acceptable behavior.

Adherents: Followers or members.

Prejudices: Hostile attitudes or negative opinions formed without sufficient knowledge or experience.

Scapegoat: Target of blame.

Ostracized: Excluded or banished from a group or society.

What happened next...

The Persian Gulf War began on January 17, 1991, and ended in a decisive victory for the U.S.-led coalition six weeks later. Although Saddam Hussein maintained control over the Iraqi government, the war left his country's military and economy in ruins. Thanks in part to the participation of Arab countries on the U.S. side, the war did not cause much of a backlash against Arabs and Muslims in American society.

A decade later, however, Arabs and Muslims living in the United States once again had reason to fear for their safety and liberty. On September 11, 2001, radical Islamic terrorists hijacked four commercial airplanes and flew them into the World Trade Center towers in New York City and the Pentagon building in Washington, D.C. The terrorist attacks claimed more than three thousand lives. U.S. government officials soon traced the terrorist plot back to a fundamentalist Islamic group called Al Qaeda, which was led by a Muslim cleric (religious leader) named Osama bin Laden. They also learned that the Taliban government of Afghanistan had sheltered and supported the organizers of the terrorist attacks.

In the immediate aftermath of September 11, many Arabs and Muslims living in the United States worried that Americans would target them for retaliation. One person who expressed such concerns was Fariba Nawa, who by this time was a graduate student and free-lance journalist living in New York City. "Americans are angry—rightly so—and want someone to blame and attack," she wrote in an essay titled "Hiding in Brooklyn." "But I shudder to think of the innocent Muslims who could be the victims of this fury.... Stereotyping and verbal attacks are not my fear anymore. The magnitude of this tragedy may provoke violence against Muslim and especially Afghan communities in this country."

Nawa was not alone in her concerns. A survey conducted by Zogby International showed that 57 percent of Muslims who attended a mosque in the United States believed that American attitudes toward Muslims and Arabs were unfavorable after September 11. In addition, 52 percent reported cases of ethnic or religious discrimination against individuals, businesses, or mosques in their communities.

"In those first days after the terrorist attacks, hundreds of cases of anti-Muslim and anti-Arab harassment, violence, and discrimination were reported to the FBI, local police agencies, and other governmental bodies," John Zogby wrote in his introduction to "In Sh'allah: Meet America's

Muslim Community." "To their credit, President George W. Bush and others such as New York City Mayor Rudolph Giuliani called upon their fellow citizens to remember this nation's highest principles and to remind all Americans that we were not at war against Islam or all Arabs."

Did you know...

- In 2002 the United States went to war in Afghanistan in order to destroy terrorist training camps and remove the Taliban government from power. U.S. troops were unable to capture Osama bin Laden during the invasion, but American forces continued to pursue him.

- As of 2004, American society continued to debate over the use of "racial profiling" in the homeland security efforts that were put in place after September 11. Racial profiling is a law enforcement technique which singles

In the days following the September 11, 2001 terrorist attacks, there were hundreds of cases of anti-Arab harassment, violence, and discrimination reported in the United States. Even Arab children, like those pictured here, experienced this mistreatment. *ACCESS. Reproduced by permission.*

out people belonging to certain ethnic groups for closer scrutiny. Some law enforcement officers say that targeting people of Arab descent saves them time and money in the fight against terrorism. But Arab and Muslim leaders argue that racial profiling is an unfair violation of their civil rights and an insult to law-abiding members of their communities.

- Many Arabs and Muslims living in the United States feel that American government policies contributed to the September 11 terrorist attacks, particularly U.S. support of Israel in its ongoing territorial dispute with the Palestinians. In the Zogby survey, 67 percent of Muslims said that the best way to wage war on terrorism was to change U.S. foreign policy in the Middle East. "I wonder if Americans know that the rage they are feeling today is what Palestinians and Muslims across the world feel every day against the American government," Nawa wrote in "Hiding in Brooklyn."

Every time there has been an attack against Americans, the government focuses on retribution and prevention, but pays little attention to changing its policies such as indifference to the loss of Palestinian lives. There is no justification for [the September 11] terrorist attacks, but increasing security at airports and catching the culprits are short-term Band-aids that will probably not stop these disasters. Reconsidering American policies and creating a consistent and fair approach to deal with other nations is a long-term solution.

For More Information

Nawa, Fariba. "Afghan Women in Exile Demand Post-Taliban Role." *Pacific News Service,* November 12, 2001. Available online at http://news.pacificnews.org/news/view_article.html?article_id=09fb66c0c1fef1d8c2e4cd57e6f68643 (accessed on March 2, 2004).

Nawa, Fariba. "Hiding in Brooklyn: Afghan American Fears for Safety." *Pacific News Service,* September 12, 2001. Available online at http://www.alternet.org/print.html?StoryID=11482 (accessed on March 2, 2004).

Ridgeway, James, ed. *The March to War.* New York: Four Walls Eight Windows, 1991.

George H. W. Bush

Excerpt from his announcement of war against Iraq

Nationally televised on January 16, 1991

At 9:00 PM on January 16, 1991, President George H. W. Bush appeared on national television to inform the American people that the United States and its allies were engaged in a war against Iraq. Most Americans had been expecting this announcement for some time. On August 2, 1990, Iraqi leader Saddam Hussein had ordered his military forces to invade the neighboring country of Kuwait. Hussein argued that Iraq had a historical claim to Kuwait's territory. He also wanted to control Kuwait's oil reserves and to gain access to Kuwait's port on the Persian Gulf. But the invasion outraged members of the international community and started a chain of events that seemed to lead inevitably toward war.

Many countries around the world criticized Husseins's actions. The United Nations Security Council passed a resolution condemning the invasion and demanding that Iraq withdraw from Kuwait. It also imposed strict restrictions on trade with Iraq in order to punish Hussein for breaking international law. Many people hoped that the sanctions would hurt the Iraqi economy and make it impossible for Hussein to continue his occupation of Kuwait.

On January 16, 1991, President George H. W. Bush appeared on national television to announce that the Persian Gulf War had begun. *Courtesy of The Library of Congress. Reproduced by permission.*

In the meantime, the United States and its allies began sending military forces to the Persian Gulf region. On November 29, the United Nations Security Council passed resolution 678, which established a deadline of midnight on January 15, 1991, for Hussein to withdraw his army from Kuwait. If Iraq continued to occupy Kuwait after the deadline, the Security Council authorized the allied coalition, made up of more than thirty-five countries, to use "all necessary means to ... restore international peace and security in the area."

During the next six weeks, a number of world leaders made frantic efforts to negotiate a peaceful solution to the crisis. But Hussein refused to withdraw his forces from Kuwait and instead moved even more troops across the border. He also began threatening to attack other nearby countries, including Israel and Saudi Arabia. As the UN deadline drew closer, the U.S. Congress held a series of debates and formally approved the use of force against Iraq. The January 15 deadline came and went without any indication that Hussein would withdraw. The following day the U.S.-led coalition launched an air war against Iraq.

The first official U.S. government announcement of the start of the war came at 7:00 PM on January 16. White House spokesman Marlin Fitzwater gave a press briefing in which he stated that "the liberation of Kuwait has begun." Two hours later President Bush made a prepared speech on national television. In this speech, which is excerpted here, Bush tells the American people that negotiations and sanctions failed to convince the Iraqi forces to leave Kuwait. He claims that the six-month Iraqi occupation took a terrible toll on the Kuwaiti people and also had negative effects on other countries around the world. He outlines the U.S. strategy, which involves using massive air strikes to destroy Iraq's offensive military capability so that it can no longer threaten its neighbors. Bush stresses that his goal is to free Kuwait rather than conquer Iraq. He places the blame for the war squarely on Saddam Hussein and says that he has no argument with the Iraqi people.

Things to remember while reading the excerpt from President Bush's announcement of war against Iraq:

- In his speech President Bush says that the Iraqi army "subjected the people of Kuwait to unspeakable atrocities [extremely cruel or brutal acts]." He is referring to the fact that thousands of people in Kuwait were arrested, tortured, or killed in the weeks following the Iraqi invasion. Iraqi soldiers randomly pulled people off the streets of Kuwait City and held them for questioning. Anyone who was suspected of resisting Iraqi rule was executed. Many witnesses reported that the Iraqi forces set up "torture centers" to intimidate and extract information from the Kuwaiti people. Iraqi soldiers also broke into thousands of private homes and businesses and stole or destroyed everything of value.

- Among the reasons President Bush provides for going to war is that Iraq's occupation of Kuwait was causing serious damage to economies around the world. The price of oil doubled to reach $40 per barrel in the months following the Iraqi invasion. This rapid price increase hit hardest in the poor countries of the developing world (also known as the Third World). As these countries struggled to industrialize, they became more dependent on oil imports than ever before. One economist estimated that every dollar increase in the price of a barrel of oil added $2 billion to a developing country's annual cost of imports. The crisis in the Persian Gulf also affected some Third World countries by cutting off the flow of income from their citizens who worked in the region. Hundreds of thousands of people from poor nations of Asia and North Africa lived in Kuwait, Saudi Arabia, and other wealthy Middle Eastern nations. They held jobs as "guest workers" and sent most of their earnings home to support their families. The rev-

Engaged: Involved.

Arab League: A political, economic, and military alliance of twenty Arab nations and the Palestine Liberation Organization (PLO).

United Nations: An international organization founded in 1945 to promote peace, security, and economic development; membership now includes most countries of the world.

Brutalized: Treated in a cruel and ruthless manner.

Resolutions: Formal expressions of will or intent.

Consent: Formal agreement.

Diplomatic activity: Attempts to negotiate a peaceful solution.

Baghdad: Capital city of Iraq.

Geneva: Capital city of Switzerland, where U.S. Secretary of State James Baker met with Iraqi Foreign Minister Tariq Aziz on January 9, 1991.

Rebuffed: Rejected or turned away.

Secretary General of the United Nations: Head of the administrative branch of the United Nations; during the Persian Gulf War this position was held by Peruvian diplomat Javier Perez de Cuellar (1920–).

enue generated by these citizens played an important role in some developing countries. Guest workers sent $400 million per year back to India, for example, and $100 million per year back to the Philippines. Finally, many guest workers fled the Persian Gulf region following Iraq's invasion of Kuwait, which left many developing nations struggling to deal with refugees.

Excerpt from President Bush's 1991 announcement of war against Iraq

*Just two hours ago, allied air forces began an attack on military targets in Iraq and Kuwait. These attacks continue as I speak. Ground forces are not **engaged**.*

*This conflict started August 2nd when the dictator of Iraq invaded a small and helpless neighbor. Kuwait—a member of the **Arab League** and a member of the **United Nations**—was crushed, its people **brutalized**. Five months ago, Saddam Hussein started this cruel war against Kuwait. Tonight, the battle has been joined.*

*This military action, taken in accord with United Nations **resolutions**—and with the **consent** of the United States Congress—follows months of constant and virtually endless **diplomatic activity** on the part of the United Nations, the United States, and many, many other countries. Arab leaders sought what became known as an Arab solution—only to conclude that Saddam Hussein was unwilling to leave Kuwait. Others traveled to **Baghdad** in a variety of efforts to restore peace and justice. Our Secretary of State, James Baker, held an historic meeting in **Geneva**—only to be totally **rebuffed**. This past weekend, in a last ditch effort, the **Secretary General of the United Nations** went to the Middle East with peace in his heart—his second such mission. And he came back from Baghdad with no progress at all in getting Saddam Hussein to withdraw from Kuwait.*

Now the 28 countries with forces in the Gulf area have exhausted all reasonable efforts to reach a peaceful resolution, have no choice but to drive Saddam from Kuwait by force. We will not fail.

As I report to you, air attacks are underway against military targets in Iraq. We are determined to knock out Saddam Hussein's nu-

clear bomb potential. We will also destroy his chemical weapons facilities. Much of Saddam's **artillery** and tanks will be destroyed. Our operations are designed to best protect the lives of all the coalition forces by targeting Saddam's vast military **arsenal.**

Initial reports from **General Schwarzkopf** are that our operations are proceeding according to plan.

Our objectives are clear. Saddam Hussein's forces will leave Kuwait. The legitimate government of Kuwait will be restored to its rightful place and Kuwait will once again be free. Iraq will eventually comply with all **relevant** United Nations resolutions. And then, when peace is restored, it is our hope that Iraq will live as a peaceful and cooperative member of the family of nations, thus enhancing the security and stability of the Gulf.

Some may ask, why act now? Why not wait? The answer is clear: The world could wait no longer. **Sanctions,** though having some effect, showed no signs of accomplishing their **objective.** Sanctions were tried for well over five months, and we and our allies concluded that sanctions alone would not force Saddam from Kuwait.

While the world waited, Saddam Hussein **systematically** raped, **pillaged**, and **plundered** a tiny nation, no threat to his own. He subjected the people of Kuwait to unspeakable **atrocities**—and among those **maimed** and murdered [were] innocent children.

While the world waited, Saddam sought to add to the chemical weapons arsenal he now possesses an **infinitely** more dangerous weapon of mass destruction—a nuclear weapon. And while the world waited, while the world talked peace and withdrawal, Saddam Hussein dug in and moved massive forces into Kuwait.

While the world waited, while Saddam stalled, more damage was being done to the fragile economies of the Third World, the emerging democracies of Eastern Europe, to the entire world, including our own economy.

The United States, together with the United Nations, **exhausted** every means at our disposal to bring this crisis to a peaceful end. However, Saddam clearly felt that by stalling and threatening and defying the United Nations he could weaken the forces **arrayed** against him.

While the world waited, Saddam Hussein met every **overture** of peace with open contempt. While the world prayed for peace, Saddam prepared for war.

Artillery: Large guns used to launch explosive shells and missiles.

Arsenal: Collection of weapons.

General Schwarzkopf: H. Norman Schwarzkopf, commander of U.S. military forces during the 1991 Persian Gulf War.

Relevant: Important to the matter at hand.

Sanctions: Trade restrictions designed to punish a country for breaking international law by harming its economy.

Objective: Goal.

Systematically: Thoroughly and methodically.

Pillaged: Looted or stole goods during a war.

Plundered: Robbed or took by force during a war.

Atrocities: Extremely cruel or brutal acts.

Maimed: Seriously wounded; crippled, or disfigured.

Infinitely: Endlessly.

Exhausted: Used up.

Arrayed: Lined up.

Overture: Proposal.

Resolute: Firm or determined.

Prevail: Win.

Intransigent: Stubborn; unwilling to compromise.

Conquest: Military defeat and capture.

Liberation: Free from the control of another country.

Thomas Paine: British-born American writer (1737–1809) who argued in support of American independence from Great Britain during the Revolutionary War (1775–83); the phrase Bush quotes is from a pamphlet called "The Crisis," published in 1776.

*I had hoped that when the United States Congress, in historic debate, took its **resolute** action, Saddam would realize he could not **prevail** and would move out of Kuwait in accord with the United Nations resolutions. He did not do that. Instead, he remained **intransigent**, certain that time was on his side....*

*We have no argument with the people of Iraq. Indeed, for the innocents caught in this conflict, I pray for their safety. Our goal is not the **conquest** of Iraq—it is the **liberation** of Kuwait. It is my hope that somehow the Iraqi people can, even now, convince their dictator that he must lay down his arms, leave Kuwait, and let Iraq itself rejoin the family of peace-loving nations.*

Thomas Paine *wrote many years ago: "These are the times that try men's souls." Those well-known words are so very true today. But even as planes of the multinational forces attack Iraq, I prefer to think of peace, not war. I am convinced not only that we will prevail, but that out of the horror of combat will come the recognition that no nation can stand against a world united. No nation will be permitted to brutally assault its neighbor.*

What happened next...

The U.S.-led attack on Iraq received the code name Operation Desert Storm. Allied warplanes flew more than one thousand sorties (one plane flying one mission) in the first fourteen hours of the war. These planes used high-tech weapons to destroy hundreds of military and industrial targets in Iraq. Although the laser-guided "smart bombs" and missiles usually hit their targets successfully, they did occasionally miss and cause casualties (people wounded or killed) among Iraqi civilians (people not involved in the war, including women and children).

Iraq offered little resistance to the allied air strikes. Most Iraqi fighter pilots chose not to fight and instead flew their warplanes to neutral (a country not favoring either side in a war) Iran. The few Iraqi air force planes that did challenge coalition forces were shot down. Hussein did strike back, however, by firing Scud missiles (Soviet-made missiles

with limited range and accuracy) into Saudi Arabia and Israel beginning on January 17. He also ordered his troops to destroy Kuwaiti oil wells and to release millions of gallons of crude oil into the Persian Gulf.

A gun is fired aboard the battleship USS *Missouri* as the first phase of the Persian Gulf War takes place along the northern Kuwaiti coast. *©Corbis. Reproduced by permission.*

On January 23 U.S. military commanders announced that the coalition forces had achieved air superiority. This meant that the allied air strikes had destroyed all of Iraq's warplanes and anti-aircraft guns, so that future air strikes could proceed at will and expect to meet with no resistance. By mid-February U.S. military leaders felt confident that the air strikes had destroyed enough of Iraq's military capability to reduce the risk to coalition ground forces (tanks and combat troops) if an allied ground attack became necessary.

On February 22 President Bush issued a deadline of noon the following day for Iraq to withdraw its troops from Kuwait. He warned that allied forces would launch a ground war if Hussein failed to meet the deadline. By this time, two thousand planes from the United States, Great Britain, France, Italy, Canada, Saudi Arabia, and Kuwait had flown more than ninety-four thousand sorties during the five-week air war.

On February 24 Bush appeared on national television once again to announce that "the liberation of Kuwait has now entered a final phase." An estimated seven hundred thousand allied troops moved into Kuwait and Iraq. They met with little resistance from the retreating Iraqi army. Three days later Bush informed the American people that "Kuwait is liberated. Iraq's army is defeated."

Did you know...

- The Bush administration's official announcements were not the first news many Americans heard about the start of the Persian Gulf War. A number of reporters for Western television stations were staying at the Al Rasheed Hotel in downtown Baghdad on January 16, 1991. They broadcast reports regarding the start of the air war against Iraq about thirty minutes before White House spokesman Marlin Fitzwater made his press briefing, and more than two hours before President Bush made his televised speech. The reporters appeared live on television to tell viewers about hearing air-raid sirens and explosions in Baghdad, and about seeing bright flashes in the sky and fires on the horizon. One British reporter stood on his balcony as a U.S. cruise missile sailed past and smashed into the Iraqi Defense Ministry building nearby. This marked the first time that the start of a war was broadcast live on television.

- On March 19, 2003, twelve years after the end of the 1991 Persian Gulf War, President George W. Bush (son of the former president) made a similar speech announcing the start of another war against Iraq. According to the younger Bush, Iraq ignored United Nations demands to disarm following the 1991 war. He believed that Saddam Hussein still possessed weapons of mass destruction and could provide such weapons to terrorists, making Iraq a significant threat to world security. "My fellow citizens, at this hour American and coalition forces are in the early stages of military operations to disarm Iraq, free its people, and to defend the world from grave danger," President George W. Bush said in his announcement of war against Iraq. He continued by saying:

Our nation enters this conflict reluctantly, yet our purpose is sure. The people of the United States and our friends and allies will not live at the mercy of an outlaw regime [government] that threatens the peace with weapons of mass murder. We will meet that threat now with our Army, Air Force, Navy, Coast Guard, and Marines, so that we do not have to meet it later with armies of firefighters and police and doctors on the streets of our cities [following a terrorist attack].

For More Information

Cipkowski, Peter. *Understanding the Crisis in the Persian Gulf.* New York: John Wiley, 1992.

Ridgeway, James, ed. *The March to War.* New York: Four Walls Eight Windows, 1991.

Peter Arnett | 5

Excerpt from his memoir **Live from the Battlefield: From Vietnam to Baghdad—35 Years in the World's War Zones**

Published in 1994

Some of the most memorable images of the 1991 Persian Gulf War came from live television coverage of the first U.S. air strikes against the Iraqi capital city of Baghdad. The bombing began in the early morning hours of January 17, 1991 (Baghdad time). Two days earlier, Iraqi leader Saddam Hussein had failed to meet a deadline set by the United Nations Security Council for withdrawing his troops from neighboring Kuwait.

A few American journalists remained in Baghdad after the deadline expired, including Peter Arnett, John Holliman, and Bernard Shaw. These reporters, who became known as the "Boys of Baghdad," faced great personal risk in order to provide live coverage of the start of the war. Their reports on the first U.S. bombing raids were broadcast on the Cable News Network (CNN) a full half-hour before American military leaders officially announced that the war had begun.

Arnett goes to Baghdad

Iraq invaded Kuwait on August 2, 1990. Countries around the world condemned Hussein's actions and called

Peter Arnett was one of the few foreign reporters to remain in Baghdad during the 1991 Persian Gulf War.
Photograph by Charles Tasnadi. AP/Wide World Photos. Reproduced by permission.

for an immediate withdrawal of Iraqi troops from Kuwait. Many of these countries then began sending military forces to the Persian Gulf region as part of a U.S.-led coalition against Iraq. In November 1990, the UN Security Council established a deadline of January 15, 1991, for Iraq to withdraw from Kuwait or face war.

During the fall of 1990, journalists from around the world rushed to the Persian Gulf to cover the military buildup and impending war. Peter Arnett was working as a CNN correspondent in Jerusalem, Israel, at this time. CNN headquarters in Atlanta, Georgia, initially asked Arnett to remain there and cover the war from Israel.

But Arnett was eager to go to Baghdad, where he could be in the middle of the action. He knew that CNN had received permission from Hussein's government to bring special communications equipment to Iraq. He also believed that CNN reporters might be allowed to remain in Baghdad after the January 15 deadline to cover the war. "I was green with envy," he recalled in *Live from the Battlefield*. "The biggest confrontation of military might since Vietnam was shaping up and CNN was to cover it live from both sides and I was stuck in a backwater."

As the deadline approached, however, many foreign journalists decided to leave Iraq for their own safety. A number of CNN reporters and technical support crew also chose to return home. But the network remained committed to covering the war from Baghdad if possible. CNN officials asked Arnett to go to Baghdad to replace some of the departing staff members. He arrived in Iraq on January 11, just four days before the UN deadline.

CNN news anchorman Bernard Shaw was already in Iraq, waiting for permission to interview Saddam. CNN correspondent John Holliman was there as well, along with producer Robert Wiener. Arnett traveled to Baghdad with Dominic ("Nic") Robertson, a young British CNN technician. Robertson managed to smuggle a $50,000 satellite telephone into Iraq. This relatively new technology would allow the CNN staff to place calls to anywhere in the world at any time.

Reporters prepare for war

Arnett and his colleagues established a base of operations at the upscale Al Rasheed Hotel in downtown Baghdad. In the days leading up to the war, the reporters were watched constantly by "minders" who worked for the Iraqi government. Their job was to escort foreign journalists around the country, keep a close eye on their activities, and make sure the information they reported to the outside world was favorable to Iraq.

Arnett and his colleagues knew that Baghdad would be a major target for coalition bombing once the war began. They took a number of steps to prepare for the start of the war. For example, their suite of rooms contained a variety of emergency supplies, including bottled water, food, flashlights, candles, matches, blankets, and portable heaters. The basement of the hotel also featured concrete bunkers that could hold hundreds of people and provide some protection against the bombing.

Arnett felt confident that the U.S. military would not target the Al Rasheed Hotel because of the journalists and civilians (people not involved in war, including women and children) inside. He knew that the American warplanes would be using "smart" bombs guided by lasers to ensure that they hit their targets. He also believed that the hotel was a strong building that could probably survive an accidental hit.

When the U.S. air strikes against Baghdad began on January 17, Arnett, Holliman, and Shaw provided live coverage from the ninth floor of the Al Rasheed Hotel. They used a four-wire phone (a special high-quality voice transmission link) to report the action to CNN headquarters in Atlanta. Their Iraqi minders took shelter in the bunkers beneath the hotel, leaving the journalists to provide uncensored reports on the start of the war. This dramatic coverage fascinated TV viewers around the world and turned the "Boys of Baghdad" into celebrities.

Things to remember while reading the excerpt from Peter Arnett's book *Live from the Battlefield*:

- The Persian Gulf War was the first major American military conflict to be broadcast live on television. The invention of satellite communications made it possible for journalists to report on the war as it happened. Millions of viewers around the world were glued to their TV sets watching Arnett and his colleagues report the allied air strikes against Baghdad on the first night of the war. These live reports gave the war an element of drama and suspense that the world had never experienced before. They set the standard for how future conflicts would be covered.

- Arnett was a veteran war correspondent who won a Pulitzer Prize for his coverage of the Vietnam War (1954–75) in 1966. Over the years he gained a reputation as a brave and resourceful reporter. He joined CNN shortly after it was founded in 1981 because he liked the network's commitment to providing twenty-four-hour continuous news coverage. Arnett's experience reporting from many war zones around the world helped prepare him for what he experienced in Baghdad on the first night of the Persian Gulf War.

- Arnett and his colleagues worked very hard and faced great danger to provide their live commentary on the start of the war. They were concerned that a stray bomb might hit the Al Rasheed Hotel and injure or kill them. They also were worried that CNN might lose their signal, especially when the Iraqi telecommunications building was hit by a bomb. Finally, they frequently had to hide from Iraqi government censors who were trying to shut down their live broadcast.

Excerpt from Live from the Battlefield

The nineteenth-century clock tower on the Baghdad railway station was barely visible in the dense early morning fog, but I could hear the bell chiming. One, two, three, four, five, six, seven, eight. It was January 16. The deadline for withdrawal had passed and Saddam Hussein had not budged....

[Most members of the foreign press corps left Baghdad once the deadline passed. But Arnett and a small CNN crew remained behind, waiting anxiously for something to happen. The coalition air strikes started early in the morning of January 17.] I was looking out the window. There was no moon in the skies over Baghdad, a "bombers' night" someone had once told me in Vietnam, when warplanes could sneak in unnoticed.

Nic [Robertson] **inclined** his head a little, did he hear planes? I told him he was dreaming. He walked across the hall to a room with open windows. Then he ran back, his face flushed.

"The dogs in the entire neighborhood are going crazy. They're barking like they're **deranged**," he shouted.

Dog radar?

In the next instant, a huge flash lit the southern sky. Nic looked like his insides had dropped into his trousers. I shook my head in disbelief. **Conventional wisdom** said that President Bush would wait a few days before he ordered the bombers in.

The **staccato** crack of guns firing into the skies confirmed that the war had begun. I glanced at my watch for history's sake: 2:32 AM....

I lurched toward the work space. The four-wire phone was humming its invitation to broadcast. Nic was already on the move, disappearing down the hallway. He had propped open every doorway between his room and the safety of the bomb shelters ten floors below.

Bernie Shaw was kneeling, gazing out the ninth-floor window as he groped for the microphone. "Come to Baghdad, come to Baghdad," he was shouting, his fingers stabbing at the control button. "Something is happening, something is happening."

My heart skipped a beat. Bernie was first with the story. But my competitive disappointment evaporated as I looked beyond him out the windows.

The glow was so red it seemed as though the sun had returned to set again. Chains of yellow lights swung across the sky as though suspended from a giant **chandelier** and I assumed they were tracer bullets from the anti-aircraft guns....

Inclined: Lifted or tilted.

Deranged: Insane.

Conventional wisdom: Generally accepted belief.

Staccato: Occurring in short bursts.

Chandelier: A decorative hanging light.

I heard Bernie call, "Peter Arnett, join me here." Atlanta was taking us live, interrupting an interview with former Defense Secretary Caspar Weinberger.

Bernie began, "The skies over Baghdad have been **illuminated**. We're seeing bright flashes going off all over the sky. Peter?"

As I pressed my face to the mike, I stuttered my own observations and talked of the "tremendous lightning in the sky, lightning-like effects."

Outside, the lights were still on in the building and the streets. The alert sirens began sounding for the first time across the city, but every Iraqi was already awake.

As John Holliman walked into the room the hotel lights went out and so did our four-wire communications signal.... All the planning. All the debate. All the money. All down the tubes. As the world beyond our windows exploded we were helpless bystanders.

[Arnett goes to assist a cameraman.] When I returned to the work space I saw Holliman crouched at the window, staring at the fiery night and talking into the four-wire microphone, which he had attached to a long cord.

"Hello, Atlanta, Atlanta. This is Holliman. I don't know whether you're able to hear me now or not, but I'm going to continue to talk to you as long as I can." Holliman had placed new batteries in the four-wire to revive it. The yellow pilot light was glowing but Atlanta was not acknowledging the signal.

Holliman placed the microphone out the window to pick up the sounds of the night. Our windows rattled. We opened the doors to connecting rooms to get a **panoramic** view of the landscape.

Then, during a break in his **monologue**, Holliman heard a response from Atlanta. They'd been listening to him for ten minutes, waiting for him to stop talking so they could break in.

John danced in **exhilaration** as a large bomb blast crashed three blocks away and shook the room. I supposed it was Saddam Hussein's **Ba'ath Party** headquarters....

[The first wave of bombing attacks ends, and Baghdad is quiet. But fifteen minutes later a new wave of air strikes begins.] I handed the microphone back to Holliman. As he took his listeners on a visual tour of the early morning cityscape, the heavens began falling in again.

Illuminated: Lit up.

Panoramic: Wide; showing every direction.

Monologue: A long, unbroken speech by one person.

Exhilaration: Excitement.

Ba'ath Party: A radical political movement founded in the 1940s with the goal of uniting the Arab world and creating one powerful Arab state. Also the political party of Iraqi leader Saddam Hussein.

Unlike Peter Arnett, most war correspondents reported on the Persian Gulf War from the desert in Saudi Arabia. ©Peter Turnley/Corbis. Reproduced by permission.

"Oh, oh. Now there's a huge fire that we've just seen due west of our position. And we just heard—whoa. Holy cow. That was a large air burst that we saw. It was filling the sky...." Holliman's eyes were bulging like his **prose.** The roar of technological war **engulfed** us.

It was my turn again. I leaned close to the microphone. The hotel was shaking with shock waves. I peered out the window and my voice died in my throat. "I think, John, that air burst took out the telecommunications center." The roar of exploding bombs rolled across us.

I tried to speak steadily but there was a high-pitched **timbre** to my voice that I couldn't **repress.** "You may hear bombs now. If you're still with us you can hear bombs now. They are hitting the center of the city." I closed my eyes and held up the microphone. Let the world hear what war sounded like. I crouched under the windowsill. The **reverberations** from multiple explosions were rattling my teeth.

I passed the microphone to Holliman, who was **speculating** that our communications link with the United States was finally

Prose: Language.

Engulfed: Surrounded and overwhelmed.

Timbre: Sound quality.

Repress: Control or prevent.

Reverberations: Series of echoes.

Speculating: Wondering or guessing.

Anchor: Studio host of a TV news program.

Superfluous: Extra; beyond what is necessary.

Laconically: Briefly or concisely.

Scooped: Beat to the release of important news.

Pentagon: Headquarters of the U.S. Department of Defense near Washington, D.C.

blasted out. *"I'm going to ask if you can still hear us in Washington and Atlanta. Are you still able to hear us?"*

Anchor *David French's voice over the crackling speaker reassured us. "John, we do still hear you. Continue. We do hear you."*

Holliman explained, "You know, when you see your main communications link to the outside world hit with a bomb you have to keep checking to make sure you're getting out."

French interrupted with confirmation from U.S. [military] headquarters in Saudi Arabia that the war had begun. "I suppose that information may be **superfluous** *to you. You're watching it," he commented* **laconically.** *We had* **scooped** *the* **Pentagon's** *press office by twenty-seven minutes on the start of the Gulf War.*

What happened next...

Arnett and his colleagues managed to continue their live broadcasts from the Al Rasheed Hotel in downtown Baghdad for seventeen hours. They periodically had to go off the air in order to hide from Iraqi government minders who wanted to shut down their broadcasts. "I was counting on the confusion of the first hours of the war to keep our broadcast window open," Arnett explained in his memoir.

> *I doubted that the Iraqi government ever intended to allow the three of us reporters to spill our unsupervised observations to a worldwide audience at such a critical time. Every step outside the hotel and every interview during the whole Gulf crisis had been supervised by Iraqi minders. The raw information we were relaying [the night of January 17] was of vital military significance.*

The "Boys of Baghdad" became part of the story on the first night of the Persian Gulf War. As their live reports for CNN were carried to countries around the world, viewers marveled at their courage and worried about their safety. They finally went off the air when the Iraqi military prohibited further live news broadcasts. By this time, Arnett felt satisfied that:

we had made the most of our unique window of opportunity. We had reported live for seventeen hours without a second of censorship. We had watched the enemy capital come under intensive attack. We had identified every target that we knew had been hit, and speculated on many that hadn't. We had said everything we wanted to about the war and Saddam Hussein, right in his own backyard. We had a thorough scoop over our competitors the night the war began.

Most other journalists left Iraq once the war started, but Arnett stayed through the entire conflict. He was escorted around the country by Iraqi officials and allowed to give televised reports of what he saw. Arnett was the only reporter to gain access to some Iraqi sites during the war. Some people criticized his reports, however, because they were all cleared by Iraqi censors. In fact, some U.S. government officials accused Arnett of supporting the Iraqis and only telling their side of the story. His most controversial report involved the destruction of a suspected chemical weapons plant by coalition bombs. His Iraqi contacts allowed him to tour the ruins of the plant, which they said had produced infant formula. Following his tour, Arnett filed reports that supported the Iraqi claims. Arnett finally left Iraq in March 1991, after the war ended.

Did you know...
- Peter Arnett was born in New Zealand in 1934. He later immigrated to the United States and became a naturalized American citizen.

- Arnett was fired from CNN in 1998 over a controversial report in which he accused the U.S. military of using chemical weapons during the Vietnam War.

- Arnett returned to Iraq in 2003 to cover the second Gulf War for the NBC television network and *National Geographic*. He once again became the center of controversy when he agreed to be interviewed on the official Iraqi government television station. In this interview, Arnett provided his analysis of the U.S. war effort. He claimed that the initial American war plan had failed and that

U.S. leaders were scrambling to come up with a new plan. U.S. government officials criticized his statements, and he was later fired by both NBC and *National Geographic*. "Clearly by giving that interview I created a firestorm in the United States and for that I am truly sorry," Arnett said afterward.

For More Information

Arnett, Peter. *Live from the Battlefield: From Vietnam to Baghdad—35 Years in the World's War Zones.* New York: Simon and Schuster, 1994.

"Peter (Gregg) Arnett." *Contemporary Authors Online.* Reproduced in *Biography Resource Center Online.* Farmington Hills, MI: Gale Group, 2003.

Wilkinson, Mark. "NBC Fires Peter Arnett over Iraqi TV Interview." *Yahoo! News,* March 31, 2003.

Anonymous Iraqi Army Lieutenant

*Excerpt from his diary during the coalition
bombing of Operation Desert Storm
January 15–February 17, 1991*

**Available on Historical Text Archives, Mississippi State
University (Web site).**

O n August 2, 1990, Iraqi leader Saddam Hussein
launched a military invasion of Kuwait. Iraqi troops oc-
cupied the tiny country on the Persian Gulf for the next six
months. Most nations around the world condemned Iraq's
actions, and more than thirty-five countries joined the U.S.-
led coalition that sent military forces to the region. The
United Nations (UN) Security Council established a deadline
of January 15, 1991, for the Iraqi army to withdraw from
Kuwait or risk an attack by coalition forces. When Hussein
failed to withdraw his troops by the deadline, the coalition
launched a series of intensive air attacks against military targets in Iraq and Kuwait.

The diary excerpt that follows begins on the day of
the UN Security Council deadline. It was written by a young
lieutenant in the Iraqi army who was part of a unit assigned
to defend al-Salman air field in southern Iraq. This air field
became a key military target of the coalition bombing raids
that began on January 17. The Iraqi lieutenant describes his
experiences during a month of coalition air attacks.

The Iraqi soldier talks about his feelings of fear and frustration during the coalition bombing raids. He witnesses the deaths of fellow soldiers on several occasions. He is nearly killed himself when low-flying coalition planes fire missiles and machine guns at Iraqi troops and tanks. He eventually becomes angry at his inability to fight back against the constant attacks.

The young soldier also expresses concern about his family and how the war will affect them. He worries about his parents and his wife and children somewhere in Iraq, as well as his brothers who are stationed in Kuwait with the Iraqi army. The lieutenant also is troubled by the fact that his younger brother has recently become eligible to be drafted into the army. He tries to send a letter to his loved ones and becomes upset when it is returned to him.

The writer of the diary is a practicing Muslim (a person who follows the religion of Islam). He appears to be a deeply religious man. He quotes from the Koran (the holy book of the Islamic religion) on several occasions, and he often calls upon God to protect him and his family. But the experiences he endures in the war eventually cause him to question his faith. By the end of the diary, the young soldier has grown very ill and has trouble performing his duties.

Things to remember while reading the excerpt from the Iraqi Army Lieutenant's diary:

- In the first diary entry, the young soldier says that he supports Hussein's decision to invade Kuwait. He believes that Iraq has a "historic right" to Kuwaiti territory. He is referring to the fact that Kuwait was a part of Iraq during the late 1800s, when most of the Middle East region was controlled by the Ottoman Empire. When Great Britain took charge of the area following World War II (1939–45), British authorities established new borders that made Iraq and Kuwait separate nations. Some Iraqis argued that Kuwait should have been included as part of Iraq. They felt that the British government had taken away land that lawfully belonged to them.

- Iraqi soldiers were not always treated well by Saddam's government. During the Persian Gulf War, many Iraqi

troops received little pay, suffered shortages of food and water, and were forced to fight against their will by threats of violence against them and their families. The Iraqi lieutenant who wrote this diary admits being hungry, thirsty, exhausted, depressed, and ill. He also recalls an incident in which some Iraqi soldiers were executed for leaving their posts without permission.

- The young soldier discusses an episode in which a flock of sheep wander into his army camp. He decides that coalition bombing raids must have killed the shepherd who was guarding the flock. He expresses outrage that the coalition bombs hit Iraqi civilians (people not involved in the war, including women and children). Although the coalition air strikes were aimed at military targets, such as air bases and nuclear and chemical weapons facilities, they sometimes missed or were mistakenly aimed at civilian targets.

A photograph of Iraqi soldiers in a military transport truck in Kuwait City one day after Iraq invaded its neighboring country. Iraqi leader Saddam Hussein believed that he had a "historic right" to Kuwaiti territory. *AFP Photo/Kuna. Getty Images. Reproduced by permission.*

Excerpt from an
Anonymous Iraqi Army Lieutenant's diary

Tuesday 15 January 1991

Leave was **suspended** today for officers and men because of the end of the **period** [granted] by the **Security Council** for Iraq to withdraw from Kuwait. We are there and it is a historic right that was stolen from us when we could do nothing. The army is in a state of total alert to prepare itself against allied and American aggression expected against our well-loved territory. I am very worried for my parents because I know what these conditions represent for them. But God is good. We wish the war had not happened, but so it has, so combat would be welcome.

Thursday 17 January 1991

"Say this: all that happens is what God has decided for us" [a quotation from the Koran, the holy book of the Islamic religion]. This morning at 2:45 A.M. I heard military aircraft. A few seconds later, the guard came in and told me in a voice **tinged** with caution, fear, and **consternation**, "Lieutenant, lieutenant, there may be bombing." I dressed quickly and then realized that the American and **Atlantic** attack against our country was starting and that the war had begun. This is war, with all that word implies. Afterwards, the enemy planes began their intensive bombing on the airfield that we have been assigned to defend, at Al-Salman in Al-Matna province.

I am very worried. Rather I am very worried for my relatives. They are all alone out there. And I know how afraid they are.

O God! Protect.
O God! Patience.
O God! Save us all.

Friday 18 January 1991

Heavy enemy bombing continues. The bombing and raids kept up all last night....

Leave: Time off from military duty.

Suspended: Temporarily stopped.

Period: The United Nations gave Iraq six weeks to withdraw from Kuwait; the deadline expired on January 15, 1991.

Security Council: The division of the United Nations charged with maintaining international peace and security. It consists of five permanent member nations (the United States, Russia, Great Britain, France, and China) and ten elected members that serve two-year terms.

Tinged: Slightly changed or affected by.

Consternation: Shock or confusion.

Atlantic: Western European.

Monday 21 January 1991

*Few enemy raids today. Our military **communiqués** say that the enemy had bombed most of the regions and provinces of Iraq with planes and missiles. I am constantly gripped by **anxiety**.*

Tuesday 22 January 1991

*Thanks be to God. Many thanks be given him. Dawn has come and no raids have taken place, at least not so far.... Now heavy raids have begun again. God protect us! [He recalls going to a bunker to tell some troops to move to a safer place.] When I got there, I found four [unexploded] bombs. The situation was very difficult, because we had to pass close by them. But God protects. What an awful sight: one of the soldiers [disturbed] one of the bombs and suddenly it exploded and the soldier disappeared and I saw two pieces of his flesh on the second storey of the bunker. **Allah aqbar**. What a horrible thing to see. I went back to the **regiment** and found the first section [of troops] at another place. They had moved to safety.*

Wednesday 23 January 1991

*Threatening weather. Time drags. We wait and watch. I am very afraid for my brothers [stationed in Kuwait]. "We have built **bulwarks** around and behind them and they see nothing" [a verse from the Koran]. O God, protect! O God, save us! The planes come back to bomb again. They were close and we could see them. "If only I had wings."*

Thursday 24 January 1991

*The raids began early. They began at about 2:30 A.M. today and have continued heavily without a let-up. I heard news that **Bassorah** has been bombed heavily. May God have come to help my relatives; I am very worried about them. How I want to see them and find out how they are! God is **beneficent**. Where are they now? God only knows. Ahhhhhh!*

Friday 25 January 1991

The raids stopped today and then started up again after sunset. Leaves had been suspended but were granted again. But that

Communiqués: Messages.

Anxiety: Overwhelming fear or nervousness.

Allah aqbar: A common expression meaning "God is great."

Regiment: Organized group of soldiers.

Bulwarks: Solid walls of defense.

Bassorah: A city in Iraq.

Beneficent: Good.

doesn't help me because only 5 percent are given leave. The important thing is that they've begun again. I sent a letter to my relatives and was so worried I forgot to ask about my children ... but I said hello to everybody. I ask God to protect them all.

Saturday 26 January 1991

Enemy air strikes continue, and I'm very worried, depressed, and bored. I think about my children.

Sunday 27 January 1991

The air strikes began this morning. I learned before noon today that I have been promoted to the rank of lieutenant and that the decision reached brigade headquarters after a delay of ... weeks. This afternoon I got back the letter I had sent to my relatives. It was returned to me because the soldier who was going to mail it didn't go on leave. I was very upset at this turn of events. My mind and my heart are with my relatives, and only my body is with the army. I very much need to see my relatives. I had a dream yesterday and it was not a good **omen** *at all.*

Monday 28 January 1991

The enemy air raids continue and I am in a [shelter]. The top of it is only tent canvas. God protect us all. After sunset, a flock of sheep came up to us. Apparently the owner of the flock had been killed in the air raids. The enemy with modern planes has launched air strikes on a shepherd. Maybe the enemy took the sheep for nuclear or chemical or **petroleum** *sheep. For shame....*

Saturday 2 February 1991

I was awakened this morning by the noise of an enemy air raid. I ran and hid in the nearby trench. I had breakfast and afterwards something **indescribable** *happened. Two enemy planes came toward us and began firing at us, in turn, with missiles, machine guns, and rockets. I was almost killed. Death was a yard away from me. The missiles, machine guns, and rockets didn't let up. One of the rockets hit and pierced our shelter, which was penetrated by* **shrapnel.** *Over and over we said, "***Allah,** *Allah, Allah." One tank*

Omen: Prediction of a future event.

Petroleum: Oil.

Indescribable: Impossible to describe.

Shrapnel: Fragments of bombs or missiles.

Allah: The name of God in the religion of Islam.

burned and three other tanks belonging to 3rd Company, which we were with, were destroyed. That was a very bad experience.

*Time passed and we waited to die. The **munitions dump** of the 68th Tank Battalion exploded. A cannon shell fell on one side of the soldiers' positions, but, thank God, no one was there. The soldiers were somewhere else. The attack lasted about 15 minutes, but it seemed like a year to me. I read chapters in the Koran. How hard it is to be killed by someone you don't know, you've never seen, and can't confront. He is in the sky and you're on the ground. Our ground resistance is magnificent. After the air raid, I gave great thanks to God and joined some soldiers to ask how each of them was. While I was doing that, another air attack began....*

Sunday 3 February 1991

*Few air raids today. The pain I've been having all the past 6 months has returned. I am sad. In the last 5 days I've eaten only a few **dates** and boiled **lentils**. What have we done to God to endure*

Iraqi women survey the damage near a house which was reportedly destroyed by a missile in a town south of Baghdad. Iraqi soldiers on the frontline worried about air raids, such as this, on their families back home. *Photograph by Murad Sezer. AP/Wide World Photos. Reproduced by permission.*

Munitions dump: Place for storing old ammunition.

Dates: A type of fruit.

Lentils: Dried beans.

Anonymous Iraqi Army Lieutenant

that? I have no news of my relatives. How can I, since I don't know what is happening to me.

What will become of me? What is happening to them? I don't know. I don't know. God protect them. How I miss my children....

Monday 11 February 1991

*Enemy planes have come back and bombed heavily. We went to the trenches or, rather, the graves. I was very upset when I heard that people born in 1973 are being drafted. That means that my brother ... will have to go into the army. He is **naive**. He can't manage by himself. He'll make a fool of himself. He's too picky about his food. Where will he find room for that in the army? And especially this army! How I wish I were with him so I could help him.*

Tuesday 12 February 1991

*I have been here for more than 35 days because leaves were canceled. I am bored and sad. This morning, I learned that 26 soldiers from our division were condemned to death for **deserting** the **front**. They were **apprehended** near **Samawa** and executed at 2nd Division headquarters. Two of them were from the 68th Tank Battalion that we were with. They were unlucky. Their shame is very great. God is good. God protects.*

Thursday 14 February 1991

*I woke up at 8 A.M. this morning and said my prayers. I couldn't make my **ablutions** with water before praying, so I had to use the sand that had fallen on me and covered me from head to foot in an enemy air raid that had been going on continuously since midnight.*

*The planes launched missiles at our positions and the tanks that were with us, believing that the tanks were missile-launching sites. Smoke and dust rose into the sky and mingled with the smell of **powder**. None of us thought we could get out of this bombardment safely. But thanks be to God. I stood because I couldn't get into the trench on account of my illness. But, thank God, I wasn't hit.*

Friday 15 February 1991

I went to field hospital ... because I was very ill. I heard that Iraq has decided to withdraw from Kuwait.

Naive: Innocent; lacking experience, wisdom, or judgment.

Deserting: Leaving military service illegally.

Front: Forward battle lines where combat takes place.

Apprehended: Caught.

Samawa: A city in Iraq.

Ablutions: Washing the body as part of a religious rite.

Powder: Explosive powder used in bombs and ammunition.

Saturday 16 February 1991

*I feel so **fatigued** that I can't breathe, and I think I am going to faint at any moment from my illness. The only thing that you can find everywhere in the world is air, and yet I can't breathe it. I can't breathe, eat, drink, or talk. I have been here for 39 days and have not yet gone on leave. The planes came and bombed Battalion headquarters. Most of the positions were destroyed and three soldiers were killed. When the planes came to bomb us, I remained standing because I can't go into the trench.*

Sunday 17 February 1991

My illness is getting worse. I am short of breath. I hurt. I have begun taking medicine; I don't know what it is for, but the main thing is to take it because I know the medicine can't cause me any more pain than I'm already enduring. The air raids have started up again.

Fatigued: Tired.

What happened next...

The diary ends on February 17, 1991. It is unclear what happened to the Iraqi army lieutenant who wrote it. He may have been killed or captured by coalition forces, or he may have been transferred to a hospital to recover from his illness.

A week later, on February 24, the U.S.-led coalition launched a dramatic ground assault to force the Iraqi troops to withdraw from Kuwait. By this time, the six-week air war had taken a devastating toll on the Iraqi forces and broken their will to fight. Like the writer of this diary, many Iraqi troops were hungry, thirsty, exhausted, ill, or suffering from wounds.

Coalition leaders expected the ground war to meet with tough resistance from Hussein's army, but they encountered very little. In fact, thousands of desperate Iraqi soldiers surrendered to the advancing coalition forces. Al-Salman air field, which this lieutenant's unit was defending, was captured by U.S. Marines early in the ground war and turned into a base for allied planes. The Iraqi army suffered a terrible defeat in the ground war, as coalition forces successfully liberated Kuwait after only one hundred hours of combat.

Did you know...

- By the end of the Persian Gulf War, coalition planes had flown 110,000 sorties (one plane flying one mission) and dropped more than 140,000 tons of bombs on targets in Iraq and Kuwait.

- Many Iraqi soldiers left diaries, letters, and other personal possessions behind when they were forced to surrender or abandon their defensive positions during the war. Some of these materials were later found by coalition troops. The diary excerpted here was discovered by a French soldier named Jacques Godelfrein, who donated it to the Historical Text Archives at Mississippi State University.

For More Information

"Diary of an Iraqi Army Lieutenant." Historical Text Archives, Mississippi State University. Available online at http://historicaltextarchive. com/sections.php?op=viewarticle&artid=85 (accessed on February 27, 2004).

Lewis, Jon E., ed. *The Mammoth Book of War Diaries and Letters: Life on the Battlefield in the Words of the Ordinary Soldier, 1775–1991.* New York: Carroll and Graf, 1999.

H. Norman Schwarzkopf

7

*Excerpt from a press briefing in which
he explained coalition military strategy*

Held in Riyadh, Saudi Arabia, on February 27, 1991

U.S. Army General H. Norman Schwarzkopf was the commander of the coalition military forces from more than thirty-five countries during the 1991 Persian Gulf War. He was primarily responsible for directing the coalition's successful attack strategy, which received the code name Operation Desert Storm. This military operation achieved its objective, forcing Iraqi troops to withdraw from neighboring Kuwait, after only six weeks of fighting. The coalition forces suffered remarkably light casualties, with around one thousand soldiers killed or wounded. Some historians have called Operation Desert Storm the most successful military operation in history.

On February 27, 1991, Schwarzkopf gave a briefing (a type of speech intended to update or inform) in the ballroom of the Hyatt Regency Hotel in Riyadh, Saudi Arabia. His one-hour speech was attended by two hundred journalists and military officials, and it was broadcast live on television in the United States and thirty other countries around the world. During his speech, which is excerpted here, Schwarzkopf described the coalition's military strategy in

As commander of the U.S.-led coalition during the 1991 Persian Gulf War, General H. Norman Schwarzkopf was primarily responsible for directing the attack strategy that forced Iraqi troops to withdraw from Kuwait after only six weeks of fighting. *Getty Images. Reproduced by permission.*

great detail. He explained exactly how the forces under his command managed to defeat the Iraqi army.

Often referring to charts, the general showed reporters how the Iraqi defenses had been positioned in Kuwait. He told them how coalition planes and missiles had hit the enemy with nearly constant bombing attacks over a period of nearly six weeks. One goal of this air war was to destroy the Iraqi army's ability to see where coalition troops were positioned. Once this goal was accomplished, Schwarzkopf explained, it allowed a large coalition attack force called VII Corps to secretly circle around behind the Iraqis and attack them from the rear. The coalition strategy completely fooled the Iraqi army, which expected the attack to come from the front. Thousands of Iraqi soldiers surrendered shortly after the ground war began, while thousands of others retreated to Iraq. Coalition forces succeeded in liberating, or freeing, Kuwait after just four days of ground combat.

Things to remember while reading the excerpt from General Schwarzkopf's press briefing:

• On February 22 U.S. President George H. W. Bush gave Iraqi leader Saddam Hussein until noon the following day to begin withdrawing his troops from Kuwait. Since there was an eight-hour time difference between Washington, D.C., and Riyadh, Saudi Arabia, the deadline was 8:00 PM on February 23 according to Saudi time. Saddam failed to withdraw by this deadline, so at 4:00 AM Saudi time on February 24, Schwarzkopf launched the coalition ground attack. He says in his speech that he pushed the launch of the ground attack forward because of forecasts of approaching bad weather, reports of Iraqi mistreatment of Kuwaiti citizens, and widespread burning of Kuwaiti oil wells by Iraqi soldiers.

- Although some fighting was still going on when Schwarzkopf gave his briefing, it was clear that the coalition was on the verge of winning the war.

Excerpt from
General Schwarzkopf's press briefing

*I promised some of you a few days ago that as soon as the opportunity presented itself, I would give you a complete rundown on what we were doing, and more important, why we were doing it— the strategy behind what we were doing. I've been asked by **Secretary Cheney** to do that this evening, so … we're going to go through a complete briefing of [Operation Desert Storm]….*

*[Schwarzkopf explains that coalition ground forces initially lined up along the Saudi border facing north into Kuwait, directly across from Iraqi defensive positions.] Basically, the problem we faced was this: When you looked at the troop numbers, they really outnumbered us about three-to-two, and when you consider the number of combat service support people we have—that's **logisticians** and that sort of thing in our armed forces—we were really outnumbered two-to-one. In addition to that, they had 4,700 tanks versus our 3,500 when the buildup was complete, and they had a great deal more artillery than we do.*

*I think any student of military strategy would tell you that in order to attack a position you should have a ratio of approximately three-to-one in favor of the attacker. In order to attack a position that is heavily dug in and **barricaded** such as the one we had here, you should have a ratio of five-to-one. So you can see basically what our problem was at that time. We were outnumbered, and … we had to come up with some way to make the difference….*

*What we did, of course, was start an extensive air campaign. One of its purposes, I told you at the time, was to isolate the Kuwaiti **theater of operations** by taking out all the bridges and supply lines that ran between [Baghdad to] the north and the [Iraqi troops in the] southern part of Iraq and Kuwait. We also conducted a very*

Secretary Cheney: U.S. Secretary of Defense Richard Cheney.

Logisticians: Soldiers who collect and transport supplies for the military.

Barricaded: Hidden behind barriers.

Theater of operations: An area where military combat takes place.

A bombed Iraqi television building. In his speech, General Schwarzkopf said that a very heavy bombing campaign was needed at the beginning of the war to reduce the number of Iraqi forces that the coalition would be facing in ground combat. ©*Francoise de Mulder/Corbis. Reproduced by permission.*

heavy bombing campaign, and many people questioned why. The reason is that it was necessary to reduce these forces down to strength that made them weaker, particularly along the front-line barrier that we had to go through.

*We continued our heavy operations out in the sea because we wanted the Iraqis to continue to believe that we were going to conduct a massive **amphibious** operation in this area....*

Amphibious: Combining land and sea operations.

*As you know, very early on we took out the Iraqi air force. We knew that he [the enemy] had very, very limited **reconnaissance** means. And therefore we took out his air force, for all intents and purposes we took out his ability to see what we were doing down here in Saudi Arabia. Once we had taken out his eyes, we did what could best be described as a "Hail Mary" play in football. I think you recall when the quarterback is desperate for a touchdown at the very end [of a game] what he does is, he steps up behind the center and all of a sudden every single one of his receivers goes way out to one flank, and they all run down the field as fast as they possibly can and into the end-zone, and he lobs the ball. In essence, that's what we did.*

*When we knew that he couldn't see us anymore, we did a massive movement of troops all the way out to the extreme west, because at that time we knew that he was still **fixed** in this area [Kuwait] with the vast majority of his forces, and once the air campaign started he would be incapable of moving out to **counter** this move, even if he knew we made it. There were some additions to Iraqi troops out in this [northern] area. But they did not have the capability nor the time to put in the barrier that had been described by Saddam Hussein as an absolutely **impenetrable** tank barrier that no one would ever get through, I believe those were his words.*

*So this was an extraordinary move. I must tell you, I can't recall any time in the **annals** of military history when this number of forces have moved over this distance to put themselves in a position to be able to attack. But what's more important, not only did we move troops out there, but we literally moved thousands and thousands of tons of fuel, of ammunition, of spare parts, of water, and of food out here into this area, because we wanted to have enough supplies on hand so that if we launched this and got into a slugfest battle, which we very easily could have gotten into, we'd have enough supplies to last for 60 days. It was a gigantic accomplishment....*

*By February 23, the [Iraqi] front lines had been **attritted** down to a point where all of these [Iraqi] units were at 50 percent [strength] or below. The **second level**—and these were really tough fighters that we were worried about—were attritted to someplace between 50 and 75 percent, although we still had the **Republican Guard**, and parts of the Republican Guard were very strong. We continued to **hit** the bridges all across this area, to make absolutely sure that no more **reinforcements** came into battle....*

This then was the morning of February 24. Our plan initially had been to do exactly what the Iraqis thought we were going to

Reconnaissance: The act of gathering information to use in military operations.

Fixed: Dug into defensive positions.

Counter: Defend against or block.

Impenetrable: Impossible to break through.

Annals: Historical records.

Attritted: Reduced in numbers or weakened.

Second level: The next layer of Iraqi defenses behind the front lines.

Republican Guard: An elite, one hundred thousand-man force that was the best-trained and best-equipped part of Iraq's army.

Hit: Bomb or destroy.

Reinforcements: Additional troops and supplies.

An American soldier is mobbed by jubilant Kuwaitis as Kuwait City is liberated from Iraqi forces. General Schwarzkopf defended the decision not to capture Iraq during the 1991 war. *Photograph by Laurent Rebours. AP/Wide World Photos. Reproduced by permission*

Feints: Mock attacks designed to distract the enemy's attention away from the true area of attack.

Penetrator: A military operation intended to break through a barrier.

Breached: Broke through.

do, and that's take them on head-on into their most heavily defended area. Also, at the same time, we launched amphibious **feints** and naval gunfire, so that they continued to think that we were going to be attacking along the coast, and therefore fixed their forces in this position. They wouldn't know what was going on. I believe we succeeded in that very well.

At four in the morning, the Marines ... launched attacks through the barrier system.... At the same time, two Saudi task forces also launched a **penetrator** through the barrier. But while they were doing that, [a French armored division] launched an overland attack to their objective—Salman airfield [in southwestern Iraq]. We were held up a little bit by the weather, but by eight in the morning, the 101st Airborne launched an air assault deep in the enemy territory to establish a forward operating base.... What we found was as soon as we **breached** these obstacles and started bringing pressure, we started getting a large number of surrenders.

We were worried about the weather. The weather, it turned out, was going to get pretty bad the next day and we were worried about launching this air assault, and we also started to have a huge number of **atrocities**—of really the most unspeakable types—committed in downtown Kuwait City, to include reports that the **desalination plant** had been destroyed. And when we heard that, we were quite concerned about what might be going on. Based upon that, and the situation as it was developing, we made the decision that, rather than wait until the following morning to launch the remainder of those forces, we would go ahead and launch those forces [VII Corps] that afternoon.

This was the situation you saw the afternoon of the 24th. The Marines continued to make great progress going through the breach in this area—and we were moving rapidly north. The task force on the east coast was also moving rapidly to the north and making very, very good progress. We launched another Egyptian-Arab force, and another Saudi force, again to make the enemy continue to think that we were doing exactly what he wanted us to do, and that was to make a headlong assault into a very, very tough barrier system. At the same time, we continued to attack with the French. We also launched an attack on the part of the entire VII Corps....

At the same time—and because of our deception plan and the way it worked, we didn't even have to worry about a barrier—the 3rd Armored Division just went right around the enemy and were behind him in no time at all. And the 1st Armored Cavalry. The 24th Mechanized Division also launched out in the far west. Once the 101st had their forward operating base established there, they went ahead and launched into the **Tigris** and **Euphrates** valleys.

There are a lot of people who are still saying that the object of the U.S. was to capture Iraq and cause the downfall of the entire country of Iraq. Ladies and gentlemen, we were 150 miles away from Baghdad and there was nobody between us and Baghdad. If it had been our intention to take Iraq, if it had been our intention to destroy the country, if it had been our intention to overrun the country, we could have done it **unopposed,** for all intents and purposes. But that was not our intention. Our intention was purely to **eject** the Iraqis out of Kuwait and destroy the military power that had come in.

Atrocities: Extremely cruel or brutal acts.

Desalination plant: A facility that converts salty seawater into drinking water.

Tigris: A major river that runs through Iraq, just east of Baghdad.

Euphrates: A major river that runs through Iraq, just west of Baghdad.

Unopposed: Without meeting any enemy resistance.

Eject: Remove by force.

What happened next...

The U.S.-led coalition declared a cease-fire a few hours after Schwarzkopf gave his briefing. Although this meant that coalition forces would stop offensive military action, the cease-fire would not be official until Iraq agreed to its terms. On March 3 General Schwarzkopf and a number of other coalition military leaders (including Major General Jabir al-Sabah, commander of the Kuwaiti forces; Lieutenant General Khalid bin-Sultan, commander of the Saudi forces; Lieutenant General Michel Rocquejeoffre, commander of the French forces; and Lieutenant General Sir Peter de la Billiere, commander of the British forces) met with eight Iraqi military officers in Safwan, Iraq. The Iraqi representatives agreed to all coalition terms for a permanent cease-fire, effectively ending the Persian Gulf War.

Did you know...

- During a question-and-answer period following his briefing, General Schwarzkopf made it clear that he did not hold a high opinion of Saddam Hussein as a military leader. "As far as Saddam Hussein being a great military strategist, he is neither a strategist, nor is he schooled in the operational arts, nor is he a tactician, nor is he a general, nor is he a soldier," he stated. "Other than that, he's a great military man."

- Another reporter asked Schwarzkopf to analyze the performance of Iraq's troops. "A great deal of the capability of an army is its dedication to its cause and its will to fight. You can have the best equipment in the world, the largest numbers in the world, but if you're not dedicated to your cause, then you're not going to have a very good army," he replied. "So I attribute a great deal of the failure of the Iraqi army to their own leadership. They committed [their troops] to a cause they did not believe in. [Captured Iraqi soldiers] are all saying they didn't want to be there, they didn't want to fight their fellow Arabs, they were lied to when they went into Kuwait. And then after they got there, they had a leadership that was so uncaring that they didn't properly feed them, didn't properly give them water, and in the end, kept them there only at the point of a gun."

For More Information

Pyle, Richard. *Schwarzkopf in His Own Words: The Man, the Mission, the Triumph.* New York: New American Library, 1991.

Schwarzkopf, General H. Norman. *It Doesn't Take a Hero.* New York: Bantam, 1992.

Samuel G. Putnam III

Excerpt from a letter to his wife describing his participation in the ground war with the U.S. Army

Letter dated February 28, 1991; reprinted in *War Letters: Extraordinary Correspondence from American Wars*, 2001

After bombing targets in Iraq and Kuwait for nearly six weeks, the U.S.-led coalition launched a major ground assault on February 24, 1991. The goal of the ground war was to force Iraqi troops to withdraw from Kuwait. Rather than simply attacking the Iraqi defensive positions from the front, however, coalition leaders came up with a daring plan to surround the Iraqi forces and attack them from the rear.

Coalition forces made it appear as if the ground attack would come from Saudi Arabia (south of Kuwait) and the Persian Gulf (east of Kuwait). In the meantime, a large coalition attack force called the VII Corps secretly moved west along the Saudi Arabia-Kuwait border and then north into Iraq. The VII Corps included two-hundred-fifty thousand allied troops, thousands of tanks and armored vehicles, hundreds of heavy artillery guns, and enough fuel, ammunition, and supplies to last them for sixty days of fighting. This huge attack force moved 500 miles around the flank of the Iraqi army.

When the ground war began, the VII Corps was involved in several intense battles. But they soon fought their way through Iraqi defenses to reach the Euphrates River, cut-

U.S. soldiers prepare to board a helicopter to take them to the Saudi Arabian border where they will face Iraqi troops during the 1991 Persian Gulf War.

Photograph by Sadayuki Mikami. AP/Wide World Photos. Reproduced by permission.

ting off the main escape route for Saddam Hussein's troops in Kuwait. Thousands of desperate Iraqi soldiers surrendered to the coalition forces as they advanced. The coalition succeeded in liberating Kuwait after only four days of fighting, and U.S. President George Bush declared a cease-fire on February 28.

U.S. Army Captain Samuel G. Putnam III was a thirty-one-year-old flight surgeon with the VII Corps. He spent the four-day ground war traveling across Iraq as a member of the 1/1 Cavalry Squadron, 1st Armored Division. On the day the fighting ended, he wrote a letter to his wife, Sharon, back home in Pennsylvania. In this letter, which is excerpted here, Putnam describes his experiences during the VII Corps' dramatic push into Iraq.

Putnam is impressed by the awesome strength of the U.S.-led force that rolled across the Iraqi desert. He talks about the overwhelming power of the American weapons, which seemed to crush Iraqi resistance fairly easily. Although the first few days of combat go extremely well, Putnam's unit eventually comes under attack. He describes the fear he felt under fire, and the change that he noticed afterward in his fellow soldiers' attitudes toward war. After spending four days in often intense combat, Putnam is exhausted and glad to be alive.

Things to remember while reading the excerpt from U.S. Army Captain Samuel G. Putnam III's letter to his wife:

- Putnam recalls an incident in which he accepted the surrender of eleven Iraqi soldiers. As the coalition ground forces advanced, Iraqi soldiers abandoned their defensive positions and surrendered to allied troops in waves. Many of these Iraqi soldiers were desperate for food and water, and some of them had been wounded in the allied air attacks. A total of around eighty thousand Iraqi troops surrendered during the war. The coalition forces did not expect so many Iraqis to surrender and were not prepared to deal with this situation. They had no way of caring for the mob of prisoners, and mass surrenders threatened to halt the progress of some units. As a result, Putnam took away the weapons of the Iraqi soldiers he encountered, then sent them off to another U.S. Army division.

- Putnam says his unit was a victim of "friendly fire." This term is used to describe situations when military forces accidentally target their weapons at their own "friendly" troops instead of at enemy troops. He believes that the bomb that wounded twenty-one American soldiers connected to VII Corps was dropped on them accidentally by fellow coalition forces. The U.S.-led coalition experienced very light casualties during the Persian Gulf War, with a total of 240 soldiers killed and 776 wounded. American casualties accounted for 148 of the dead and 458 of the wounded. Military analysts claim that around one-third of these casualties were the result of friendly fire.

- Putnam closes his letter by describing oil fires on the horizon. Retreating Iraqi forces set fire to hundreds of Kuwaiti oil wells at the end of the Persian Gulf War. These huge blazes filled the air with thick, greasy, black smoke that blocked the sun over parts of the Middle East. The fires burned up millions of barrels of Kuwaiti oil and polluted the air across the Gulf region. Putting the fires out required seven months of expensive and dangerous efforts by international firefighting teams.

Excerpt from Captain Putnam's letter to his wife

Dear Sharon:

It's great to be here, even if this place is windy, dusty, and ugly—it's just great to be able to write a letter after the past 4 days.

We're now in southeastern Iraq, about 12 miles west of the Kuwaiti border. It was a truly incredible trip to this spot, which I'll tell you about from the beginning.

*On [February] the 24th, at about 8 AM, we started moving north from our last holding area in Saudi Arabia. We've known for about 4 weeks what our mission was—to go into Iraq and **outflank** their forces, focusing in on the **Republican Guards**....*

*We thought this would be our first big battle day. We thought we'd be getting shot at as we moved north that day, but instead we ran into a bunch of surrendering Iraqi soldiers. The **spot reports** started slow, maybe 3 EPW's (Enemy Prisoners of War), then 7, then 15, then 60, then 120 Iraqis surrendering. There were a bunch at a **bunker** complex that was targeted for **artillery,** so we had to get them out before our artillery could blast it. It stopped us for a couple hours, so I stood up on the aid station and watched the entire 1st Armored Division pull up behind us—it was incredible. Thousands of vehicles rolling across the desert. It visually showed me what a feat it was getting all this stuff here—and that [was] just one division out of the 8 that the army has here. A herd of camels got caught up in the movement and were totally **perplexed**—didn't know which way to go.*

*Back to the EPW's—they knew exactly how to surrender, thanks to the **leaflets** that our air force dropped on them. They had no desire to die for **Saddam**. I saw lines of them, hands over their heads, waving anything white that they could find. One guy was dancing*

Outflank: Circle around.

Republican Guards: An elite, one hundred thousand-man force that was the best-trained and best-equipped part of Iraq's army.

Spot reports: Reports passed back from other vehicles in the division.

Bunker: A protective chamber dug into the ground.

Artillery: Large, cannon-like weapons used to launch bombs and missiles.

Perplexed: Confused.

Leaflets: Pieces of paper containing Arabic messages encouraging Iraqi troops to surrender.

Saddam: Iraqi leader Saddam Hussein.

with a white sheet over his head. One group had a dog surrendering with them. They looked pretty hurting—torn up uniforms, thin, many without shoes. They just left their weapons sitting on the ground. We picked up so many of them that we stopped stopping for them and just pointed them south—let someone else in the division pick them up.

Our troops made a bit of contact with Iraqi troops not willing to give up—but they blew up the vehicles and took care of that. None of our guys were injured. The day ended about 70 miles into Iraq....

The next day we moved out at first light. The **terrain** changed dramatically—it was hilly with lots of small scraggly bushes and more camels. We went through a large **Bedouin** camp. I wonder what they were thinking as this division rolled through camp....

By nightfall we were at our **objective** that was supposed to take $4\frac{1}{2}$ days to reach. Things were going so well that we kept going. We were still the furthest unit into Iraq, and moving northeast towards Kuwait, we started to pass more enemy positions with blown up tanks and unexploded bombs and mines that we had to avoid. Everyone did avoid them.

Further on that night we started to hear and see a lot of boom-booms to our south. That was the Republican Guards fighting our 3rd Armored Division. Our guns wiped them out that night. That's also when our artillery started firing from behind us right over our heads. I was a bit nervous about a **round** falling short—but it didn't happen. At about 11:30 PM we stopped to let our artillery **prep** the battlefield in front of us. Our troops were sending **mortar** on a road to our north, artillery was going off to my west, there was a major battle to our south. I saw a vehicle blow up and fly about 100 feet into the air—and to our east were the Republican Guards that we were going after—the Medina division. Every direction I turned there were explosions. Our vehicles were lined up in columns, mine being the last vehicle of our column. I was standing outside, when I saw something fire into a hill not 200 feet from me. I dove behind my **humvee** along with 2 other guys—we were sure we were getting shot at. We had our weapons out, ready to shoot at anything that moved. I thought the worst, but it turned out one of our own **Bradleys** had fired that shot at a bunker near us. Scared by our own troops.

We moved a little further after the artillery **barrage**, then stopped for another one. I can't describe to you the power that you feel when artillery goes off anywhere nearby. The earth shakes, your body vi-

Terrain: Characteristics of the land.

Bedouin: A nomadic Arab people that live in the deserts of North Africa and the Middle East.

Objective: Goal or target.

Round: An explosive artillery shell.

Prep: Prepare.

Mortar: An explosive shell fired from a large cannon.

Humvee: Nickname for the rugged truck used by U.S. troops (short for High-Mobility, Multi-purpose Wheeled Vehicles, or HMMWV).

Bradleys: Bradley fighting vehicles (a type of U.S. military vehicle that had armor and weapons but was smaller than a tank).

Barrage: Artillery fire designed to screen and protect friendly troops.

An American soldier takes aim at Iraqi troops while in the desert during Operation Desert Storm. Captain Samuel Putnam describes such a scene in a letter he wrote to his wife during the war. *©Yves Debay; The Military Picture Library/Corbis.*

Elite: Highly trained and prestigious.

Seized: Took away.

Disheveled: Messy or rumpled.

Resounding: Loud and emphatic.

brates, the sound is deafening. I watched as these rockets were being fired directly behind me—coming right at me and over my head, hitting about 10 miles to our front. They were beautiful to watch, but it must be hell on earth to be anywhere near where they land.

Most of our guys were sleeping at this stop, but I stayed awake and kept my eyes open to our rear. I wasn't going to take any chances. I saw about 10 people coming over a hill with their hands over their heads—figured they were Iraqis surrendering. I rounded up a few guys with M-16 rifles and drove over to them. It turned out they were 11 soldiers from the Tawakalna division of the Republican Guard—supposedly the most **elite** forces, surrendering to me. My guys **seized** their weapons and searched them. They were thin, **disheveled,** cold and dirty. I asked if any of them spoke English and I got a **resounding** "no" from most of them. I laughed at that and most of them responded with a nervous chuckle. I'm sure they were worried that we might just shoot them. We put all their weapons in my humvee and pointed them west—towards the rest of the division following us. They were a little hesitant to walk away—I think they thought we would shoot them. Eventually they walked. I was left with 7 AK-47's, Soviet-made assault rifles. I got a picture of me holding them all, then **Mascellino** and I buried them. Now I can boast about how I single-handedly captured 11 enemy soldiers....

We stopped again about 3 AM. Everyone was tired but **ecstatic** that things were going so well. It seemed to good to be true—and it was. We heard a loud "crack"—much closer and different sounding than the ones we'd been hearing the last 2 days. Mascellino and I jumped out of our humvee and beelined for the nearest armored vehicle—an ambulance 2 up from me. As I ran up I twisted my ankle and limped towards the ambulance. I saw multiple explosions very close—right in front of me. I heard guys screaming and saw people running as I dove into the ambulance.

It stopped soon after I got in. We had been attacked by someone, somehow, somewhere—no one knew where it came from. I hobbled out and heard we had a lot of **casualties** at the TOC (tactical operations center) where about 100 soldiers live. I drove over there and saw guys laying out all over the place. I went to each one and checked them out—we had 21 casualties, but no one had a life-threatening injury. It was a miracle. The artillery that hit us exploded over our head, where it shoots out a bunch of little bomblets that then explode when they hit the ground. They send **shrapnel** in all directions. We dressed all the wounds, sorted the patients, and put guys on ambulances who couldn't walk....

We were incredibly lucky. With all that shrapnel flying around, no one had any vital organs or eyes pierced. Someone was definitely watching over us then....

That scene totally changed the attitude of the **squadron**. Immediately, we all realized what war really meant, and everyone hated it. I have never been as scared as when that stuff exploded. Since then, everyone wore their **frag** vest (body armor) and most slept in armored vehicles. We all jump a bit more when we hear explosions.

We still don't know where that came from—but it was most likely from our own guys. **Friendly fire** that wasn't.

We moved up a few more miles yesterday morning, then stopped and let the division pass us by. They battled all day yesterday with tanks, Apache helicopters, artillery, and jets going after the retreating Iraqis. By last night I was delirious—I hadn't slept in 38 hours. I crashed in the ambulance and slept a solid 10 hours, woken

Mascellino: Name of a fellow U.S. soldier.

Ecstatic: Thrilled.

Casualties: Killed or wounded soldiers.

Shrapnel: Fragments of bombs or missiles.

Squadron: Military unit.

Frag: Short for "fragment"; clothing designed to protect soldiers from shrapnel or shell fragments.

Friendly fire: A term used when military forces accidentally shot their weapons at their own troops instead of at enemy troops.

up *intermittently* by the explosions around us, hoping that they were outgoing and not incoming.

This morning I woke up and heard the second *best news in my life—**Pres. Bush** announcing a cease-fire. I was working on patients later this morning when I heard the* best *news in my life—that Iraq had accepted the cease-fire terms. Hopefully that's it, but I won't believe it for sure until I'm out of here.*

The sun's now setting and to the east I can see the red glow of an oil field burning under dark clouds, with a full moon rising above the clouds. It's beautiful....

Intermittently: Once in a while.

Pres. Bush: U.S. President George Bush.

What happened next...

The official end of the Persian Gulf War came on April 3, 1991, when the United Nations Security Council passed Resolution 687. This resolution lifted economic sanctions (trade restrictions designed to punish a country for breaking international law by harming its economy) on food shipments to Iraq, but left other trade restrictions in place until Iraq met a number of requirements. For example, Iraq was required to respect its border with Kuwait and to pay for damages caused by its occupation. The resolution also required Iraq to destroy or remove all of its biological, chemical, and nuclear weapons and provided for UN inspectors to monitor its progress.

Once the war ended, U.S. troops returned home to triumphant celebrations. In the meantime, both Kuwait and Iraq struggled to overcome the terrible destruction the war had caused. The Iraqi people rose up in rebellion against Saddam Hussein's weakened government after the war, but Hussein used the remains of his military to violently crush the uprisings.

Did you know...

- Doctor Putnam retired from the military following his service in the Persian Gulf War. He returned home to

Pennsylvania and entered private medical practice as a radiologist (a doctor who uses X rays to diagnose and treat disease).

• The letter Putnam wrote to his wife at the end of the Persian Gulf War was one of two hundred letters included in a 2001 collection called *War Letters: Extraordinary Correspondence from American Wars.* The editor of this book, Andrew Carroll, selected the letters from more than fifty thousand he received through the Legacy Project. Founded in 1998, the Legacy Project is an effort to honor U.S. military veterans by collecting and preserving their wartime correspondence, from the American Civil War (1861–65) to the present. For more information, visit http://www.warletters.com.

For More Information

Carroll, Andrew, ed. *War Letters: Extraordinary Correspondence from American Wars.* New York: Scribner, 2001.

Brent Scowcroft

Excerpt from his editorial "Don't Attack Saddam"

Published in the *Wall Street Journal*, August 15, 2002

The United Nations (UN) agreement that officially ended the 1991 Persian Gulf War required Iraq to destroy all of its biological, chemical, and nuclear weapons. In the decade after the war ended, however, Iraqi leader Saddam Hussein refused to honor the terms of this peace agreement. He consistently failed to cooperate with the UN weapons inspectors sent to monitor Iraq's progress in destroying its weapons of mass destruction. In fact, Hussein kicked the inspectors out of Iraq in 1998.

From the time he took office in January 2001, President George W. Bush vowed to adopt a tougher policy toward Iraq than his predecessor, Bill Clinton. The terrorist attacks that struck the United States on September 11, 2001, only increased Bush's determination to eliminate Hussein as a potential threat to world security.

Immediately following the terrorist attacks, Bush launched a global war on terrorism that initially focused on known terrorist groups. In his January 2002 State of the Union address, he announced his intention to expand the fight against terrorism to include nations that harbored terrorists or provided weapons, training, or financial support for their activities. Iraq was one of the countries he accused of supporting terrorists. Bush claimed that Iraq posed a threat to world security because it could provide terrorists with weapons of mass destruction.

Over the next six months, officials in the Bush administration began talking about the importance of "regime change" in Iraq, or removing Saddam Hussein's government from power. In addition, the U.S. Department of Defense began leaking to the press possible strategies for a military invasion of Iraq. Many people expressed uneasiness about the Bush administration's apparent determination to invade Iraq. As it became increasingly clear that Bush was considering going to war to remove Hussein from power, some U.S. lawmakers and world leaders began speaking out against the idea.

One of the most attention-grabbing criticisms of Bush's policy came from retired U.S. Air Force General Brent Scowcroft. Scowcroft was one of the Republican Party's most respected experts on international affairs. He served as national security advisor to Bush's father, President George H. W. Bush, and was a close friend of the Bush family.

Scowcroft disagreed with the Bush administration's push for an invasion of Iraq. He felt that military action in Iraq would distract from the war on terrorism and potentially create other foreign policy problems. Scowcroft expressed his feelings on August 4, 2002, during an appearance on the CBS News program "Face the Nation." He warned that an invasion of Iraq "could turn the whole [Middle East] region into a cauldron [kettle full of boiling liquid], and thus destroy the war on terrorism." Scowcroft followed up with an editorial called "Don't Attack Saddam," which was published in the *Wall Street Journal* on August 15, 2002.

Things to remember while reading the excerpt from "Don't Attack Saddam":

- One of the Bush administration's main reasons for removing Saddam Hussein from power was to prevent the Iraqi leader from providing weapons of mass destruction to terrorist groups. In his editorial, Scowcroft argues that there is no evidence of a link between Hussein and the terrorists.

He also questions the idea that Hussein would provide weapons of mass destruction to terrorist groups. Finally, he claims that attacking Iraq would distract from the global war on terrorism and perhaps even make the situation worse. He believes that toppling Hussein could destabilize the Middle East, alienate the Arab world, and reduce international cooperation in the war on terrorism.

- Scowcroft warns that attacking Hussein would go against international sentiment and lack United Nations support. He also says that an invasion of Iraq, followed by a long-term military occupation of the country, would be tremendously expensive. He urges the Bush administration to adopt a more cautious approach and push for tougher weapons inspections instead.

Although a close friend of the Bush family, former U.S. National Security Advisor Brent Scowcroft criticized George W. Bush's plan to go to war with Iraq in order to remove Iraqi leader Saddam Hussein from power. *Photograph by Alex Wong. Getty Images. Reproduced by permission.*

Excerpt from Brent Scowcroft's editorial "Don't Attack Saddam"

Our nation is presently engaged in a debate about whether to launch a war against Iraq. Leaks of various strategies for an attack on Iraq appear with regularity. The Bush administration vows **regime change***, but states that no decision has been made whether, much less when, to launch an invasion.*

It is beyond dispute that Saddam Hussein is a **menace***. He terrorizes and brutalizes his own people. He has launched war on two of his neighbors. He devotes enormous effort to rebuilding his military forces and equipping them with weapons of mass destruction. We will all be better off when he is gone.*

Regime change: Removing Saddam Hussein's government from power.

Menace: Threat or danger.

War on terrorism: A U.S.-led, global effort to identify and eliminate terrorists that pose a threat to world security.

Strategic objective: Long-term goal.

Scant: Very little.

Sept. 11 attacks: Coordinated attacks in which terrorists hijacked commercial airliners and crashed them into the World Trade Center in New York City and the Pentagon in Washington, D.C., on September 11, 2001.

Incentive: Reason.

Make common cause: Work together in a joint effort.

Blackmail: Using threats to achieve a desired outcome.

Dictatorial aggressor: A person who rules with absolute power and uses that power to threaten others.

Deter: Discourage or prevent.

Intervening: Becoming involved.

Designs: Plans.

Preeminent: Primary or most important.

Underscored: Emphasized.

Counterterrorist campaign: A U.S.-led, global effort to identify and eliminate terrorists that pose a threat to world security.

*That said, we need to think through this issue very carefully. We need to analyze the relationship between Iraq and our other pressing priorities—notably the **war on terrorism**—as well as the best strategy and tactics available were we to move to change the regime in Baghdad.*

*Saddam's **strategic objective** appears to be to dominate the Persian Gulf, to control oil from the region, or both. That clearly poses a real threat to U.S. interests. But there is **scant** evidence to tie Saddam to terrorist organizations, and even less to the **Sept. 11 attacks**. Indeed Saddam's goals have little in common with the terrorists who threaten us, and there is little **incentive** for him to **make common cause** with them.*

*He is unlikely to risk his investment in weapons of mass destruction, much less his country, by handing such weapons to terrorists who would use them for their own purposes and leave Baghdad as the return address. Threatening to use these weapons for **blackmail**—much less their actual use—would open him and his entire regime to a devastating response from the U.S. While Saddam is thoroughly evil, he is above all a power-hungry survivor.*

*Saddam is a familiar **dictatorial aggressor**, with traditional goals for his aggression. There is little evidence to indicate that the United States itself is an object of his aggression. Rather, Saddam's problem with the U.S. appears to be that we stand in the way of his ambitions. He seeks weapons of mass destruction not to arm terrorists, but to **deter** us from **intervening** to block his aggressive **designs**.*

*Given Saddam's aggressive regional ambitions, as well as his ruthlessness and unpredictability, it may at some point be wise to remove him from power. Whether and when that point should come ought to depend on overall U.S. security priorities. Our **preeminent** security priority—**underscored** repeatedly by the president—is the war on terrorism. An attack on Iraq at this time would seriously jeopardize, if not destroy, the global **counterterrorist campaign** we have undertaken.*

The United States could certainly defeat the Iraqi military and destroy Saddam's regime. But it would not be a cakewalk. On the contrary, it undoubtedly would be very expensive—with serious consequences for the U.S. and global economy—and could as well be bloody. In fact, Saddam would be likely to conclude he had nothing left to lose, leading him to unleash whatever weapons of mass destruction he possesses…. Finally, if we are to achieve our strategic

A hijacked plane prepares to crash into the World Trade Center during the September 11 terrorists attacks on the United States. In his editorial titled "Don't Attack Saddam," Brent Scowcroft said that there was very little evidence to tie Iraqi leader Saddam Hussein to terrorists and to these attacks. *Photograph by Carmen Taylor. AP/Wide World Photos. Reproduced by permission.*

objectives in Iraq, a military campaign very likely would have to be followed by a large-scale, long-term **military occupation.**

But the central point is that any campaign against Iraq, whatever the strategy, cost, and risks, is certain to **divert** us for some **indefinite** period from our war on terrorism. Worse, there is a **virtual consensus** in the world against an attack on Iraq at this time. So long as that **sentiment** persists, it would require the U.S. to pursue a virtual go-it-alone strategy against Iraq, making any military op-

Military occupation: Control of an area by a foreign army.

Divert: Distract or turn aside.

Indefinite: Unknown.

Virtual consensus: Near total agreement.

Sentiment: Feeling or belief.

Degradation: Reduction or scaling back.

Intelligence: Information gathered through spying activities.

Dire: Serious.

Israeli-Palestinian conflict: A longstanding political conflict between the Jewish state of Israel and the Arab people known as Palestinians. The creation of Israel in 1948 displaced thousands of Palestinians from their ancient homeland. Since then the Palestinians, with the support of surrounding Arab countries, have fought to reclaim lost territory and establish an independent Palestinian state.

Muslim: Followers of the religion of Islam.

Destabilize: Cause to fall apart and lose power.

Implicated: Involved in or connected with.

United Nations Security Council: The division of the United Nations charged with maintaining international peace and security. It consists of five permanent member nations (the United States, Russia, Great Britain, France, and China) and ten elected members that serve two-year terms.

Regime: Program.

Opined: Expressed an opinion.

Casus belli: A Latin phrase meaning "cause of war."

erations correspondingly more difficult and expensive. The most serious cost, however, would be to the war on terrorism. Ignoring that clear sentiment would result in a serious **degradation** in international cooperation with us against terrorism. And make no mistake, we simply cannot win that war without enthusiastic international cooperation, especially on **intelligence.**

Possibly the most **dire** consequences would be the effect in the region. The shared view in the region is that Iraq is principally an obsession of the U.S. The obsession of the region, however, is the **Israeli-Palestinian conflict.** If we were seen to be turning our backs on that bitter conflict—which the region, rightly or wrongly, perceives to be clearly within our power to resolve—in order to go after Iraq, there would be an explosion of outrage against us. We would be seen as ignoring a key interest of the **Muslim** world in order to satisfy what is seen to be a narrow American interest....

The results could well **destabilize** Arab regimes in the region, ironically facilitating one of Saddam's strategic objectives. At a minimum, it would stifle any cooperation on terrorism, and could even swell the ranks of the terrorists. Conversely, the more progress we make in the war on terrorism, and the more we are seen to be committed to resolving the Israel-Palestinian issue, the greater will be the international support for going after Saddam.

If we are truly serious about the war on terrorism, it must remain our top priority. However, should Saddam Hussein be found to be clearly **implicated** in the events of Sept. 11, that could make him a key counterterrorist target, rather than a competing priority, and significantly shift world opinion toward support for regime change.

In any event, we should be pressing the **United Nations Security Council** to insist on an effective no-notice inspection **regime** for Iraq—any time, anywhere, no permission required. On this point, senior administration officials have **opined** that Saddam Hussein would never agree to such an inspection regime. But if he did, inspections would serve to keep him off balance and under close observation, even if all his weapons of mass destruction capabilities were not uncovered. And if he refused, his rejection could provide the persuasive **casus belli** which many claim we do not now have. Compelling evidence that Saddam had acquired nuclear-weapons capability could have a similar effect.

In sum, if we will act in full awareness of the intimate relationship of the key issues in the region, keeping counterterrorism as our fore-

Brent Scowcroft

Brent Scowcroft is one of the Republican Party's most respected foreign policy experts. A retired U.S. Air Force lieutenant general, he served as national security advisor to Presidents Gerald R. Ford and George H. W. Bush.

Scowcroft was born into a Mormon family in Ogden, Utah, on March 19, 1925. He graduated from the U.S. Military Academy at West Point, New York, in 1947, and received a commission as an officer in the U.S. Air Force. He continued his education, earning a master's degree in international relations in 1953 and doctorate in the same field in 1967 from Columbia University.

Scowcroft initially trained to be a fighter pilot in the air force, but he had to quit flying after suffering serious injuries in a plane crash. He assumed a variety of roles during his twenty-nine-year military career, including that of teacher at West Point as well as at the U.S. Air Force Academy in Colorado Springs, Colorado. In 1968 he took a position with the U.S. Department of Defense in Arlington, Virginia. Two years later he served as a military aide to President Richard Nixon during his historic trip to China. It marked the first time an American president had visited Communist China, and it was part of a successful effort to open diplomatic relations between the two countries.

Scowcroft then became Nixon's deputy national security advisor, working for Henry Kissinger. He was promoted to national security advisor by Ford in 1975. It was at this time that he retired from the air force with the rank of lieutenant general. When Democrat Jimmy Carter took office as president in 1977, Scowcroft joined the private sector and worked for Kissinger and Associates international consulting firm in New York. He resumed his position as national security advisor under the elder George Bush in 1989.

Since leaving public service in 1992, Scowcroft has served on a number of corporate boards. He also is the founder and president of The Scowcroft Group, an international business consulting firm. He is married and has one daughter.

most priority, there is much potential for success across the entire range of our security interests, including Iraq. If we reject a comprehensive perspective, however, we put at risk our campaign against terrorism as well as stability and security in a vital region of the world.

What happened next...

Scowcroft's criticism proved embarrassing to the Bush administration. The article received a great deal of attention from the media and started an intense debate about the wisdom of attacking Iraq. Scowcroft seemed to express the views of many people who had reservations about U.S. leaders' swift movement toward war.

Following the appearance of Scowcroft's editorial, members of the Bush administration rushed to control the damage. President Bush, who was vacationing at his Texas ranch at the time, released a statement the following day. "I am aware that some very intelligent people are expressing their opinions about Saddam Hussein and Iraq," he said. "I listen very carefully to what they have to say."

Over the next several days, the Bush administration increased its efforts to sway public opinion toward its position. On August 26, for example, Vice President Dick Cheney presented the administration's case for war in a speech before the National Convention of the Veterans of Foreign Wars. Cheney even quoted several phrases from Scowcroft's article in making his argument. "I am familiar with the arguments against taking action in the case of Saddam Hussein," he noted.

> Some concede [admit] that Saddam is evil, power-hungry, and a menace—but that, until he crosses the threshold of actually possessing nuclear weapons, we should rule out any preemptive action. That logic seems to me to be deeply flawed. The argument comes down to this: yes, Saddam is as dangerous as we say he is, we just need to let him get stronger before we do anything about it.

Cheney argued that immediate action was necessary because Iraq posed a serious threat to world security. "Deliverable weapons of mass destruction in the hands of a terror network, or a murderous dictator, or the two working together, constitutes as grave a threat as can be imagined," he stated. "The risks of inaction are far greater than the risk of action." He also insisted that regime change would free the Iraqi people from a brutal dictator and lead to peace and stability in the Middle East.

The Bush administration continued to make its case for war over the next six months. But it failed to change international opinion or convince the United Nations to support an invasion of Iraq. Despite the lack of world support, the United States attacked Iraq in March 2003. The war succeeded in removing Hussein from power after only three weeks of fighting, and President Bush declared an end to major combat operations in Iraq on May 1.

After the war ended, however, the situation in Iraq lent support to some of Scowcroft's arguments. The war was very expensive and strained relations between the United States and some of its longtime allies. U.S. troops struggled to maintain security in the face of Iraqi resistance, and a massive search failed to uncover any weapons of mass destruction in Iraq. These developments prompted many critics to claim that the Bush administration should have waited to gather more reliable information before starting a war.

Did you know...

- Brent Scowcroft was the national security advisor to President George H. W. Bush during the 1991 Persian Gulf War.

- Scowcroft also acted as a mentor to Condoleezza Rice, who was President George W. Bush's national security advisor during the 2003 Iraq War. But he and Rice had a difference of opinion about the threat posed by Saddam Hussein. On the same day that Scowcroft published his editorial criticizing the Bush administration's policy toward Iraq, Rice defended the policy on BBC Radio. She called Hussein "an evil man who, left to his own devices, will wreak havoc again on his own population, his neighbors, and—if he gets weapons of mass destruction and the means to deliver them—all of us." She also insisted that "we certainly do not have the luxury of doing nothing."

For More Information

"Brent Scowcroft." Available online at http://www.scowcroft.com (accessed on March 5, 2004).

Purdum, Todd S., and the staff of the *New York Times*. *A Time of Our Choosing: America's War in Iraq*. New York: Times Books, 2003.

Scowcroft, Brent. "Don't Attack Saddam." *Wall Street Journal*, August 15, 2002. Available online at http://ffip.com/opeds081502.htm (accessed on March 5, 2004).

Sifry, Micah L., and Christopher Serf, eds. *The Iraq War Reader*. New York: Simon and Schuster, 2003.

Anne Garrels

Excerpt from her coverage of the fall of Baghdad

**Published in her memoir *Naked in Baghdad:*
*The Iraq War as Seen by NPR's Correspondent***

Baghdad, the capital of Iraq and center of Saddam Hussein's government, was the primary target of the U.S.-led coalition from the beginning of the 2003 Iraq War. On March 21 U.S. military leaders launched the "shock and awe" bombing campaign against Iraqi government and military targets in Baghdad. During that first night alone, bombs exploded in the city every ten seconds for three hours. By early April U.S. tanks reached the outskirts of Baghdad and began battling Iraqi forces for control of the city. After several days of intense fighting, Baghdad fell to U.S. troops on April 9.

Anne Garrels, a foreign correspondent for National Public Radio (NPR), was one of only sixteen American journalists, and the only broadcast journalist, to remain in Baghdad during the war. "As the deadline for the bombing ticked down, we realized that there were only 16 of us left, and that included print reporters, photographers—that was it!" Garrels recalled in an NPR interview. "It was a tiny group, and it was a very intimate experience. And obviously for NPR, it was a seminal moment because we were the broadcast voice from Baghdad."

Anne Garrels was only one of sixteen journalists, and the only broadcast journalist, to remain in Baghdad during the 2003 Gulf War. *Photograph by Vince Bucci. AP/Wide World Photos. Reproduced by permission.*

An experienced war correspondent, Garrels provided compelling reports from the middle of the action for the duration of the conflict. She braved bombs, snipers, and the constant threat of arrest by the Iraqi government. She became the voice of the war in the minds of thousands of listeners. Her broadcasts often focused on the war's impact on the people of Baghdad. She received unusually consistent access to ordinary Iraqis thanks to her trusted Iraqi assistant, Amer, who served as her eyes and ears on the streets of the city.

The following excerpt begins with Garrels's description of the battle for Baghdad that took place on April 8. She watches the fight for control of Hussein's Republican Palace from the balcony of her room in downtown Baghdad's Palestine Hotel. Later that night, the Palestine Hotel is fired upon by a U.S. tank. Two international news photographers are killed in the attack. U.S. military leaders later claimed that the tank responded to sniper fire coming from the hotel, but Garrels and the other journalists present did not hear any gunfire. Garrels also points out that it was common knowledge that the hotel served as the headquarters for visiting journalists.

In the second part of the excerpt, Garrels describes the changed atmosphere in Baghdad on April 9. The Iraqi resistance suddenly seems to disappear, and American tanks and troops move freely through the city streets. Garrels also covers the chaos and looting that follow the fall of Baghdad. She notes that the Iraqi people she encounters seem to have mixed feelings about the presence of U.S. troops in their capital. Some express gratitude at being freed from Hussein's rule, while others express fear or resentment toward American occupation forces. Finally, Garrels mentions that the outcome of the war leaves a lingering question in the minds of many Iraqi citizens: "Where do we go from here?"

Things to remember while reading the excerpt from Anne Garrels's coverage of the fall of Baghdad:

- The foreign journalists in Baghdad were watched carefully by Iraqi government officials known as "minders." The minders accompanied journalists wherever they went and tried to control what they saw and who they talked to. On the morning of April 9, Garrels notices that all of the minders have vanished from the Palestine Hotel. She also finds that many Iraqi troops have abandoned their posts overnight.

- Garrels makes her broadcasts from Baghdad with the help of a satellite telephone that she secretly brought into the country. The Iraqi government prohibited reporters from using such equipment except under the watchful eye of minders. Iraqi authorities frequently searched journalists' hotel rooms. Reporters found with illegal phones were either kicked out of Iraq or arrested as spies by Hussein's regime.

Excerpt from
Anne Garrels's memoir Naked in Baghdad

April 8, 2003

*The battle for the center of Baghdad begins before dawn within the sprawling gardens of Saddam Hussein's **Republican Palace**. The fighting takes place behind a curtain of date trees, but I can track the progress by watching the **tracers**, smoke, and flares gradually shift as American tanks repel an Iraqi assault. The tanks then move out of the palace compound into the city's open streets. Eventually two tanks move onto and hold one of the main bridges spanning the river. For more than seven hours the palace grounds **resound** with **artillery**, rockets, **mortars**, and tank guns backed by the vicious **strafing** of an **A-10 Warthog**. The plane moves slowly above the hotel and then lets rip on the Planning Ministry with volleys of cannon rounds—they turn the building into flaming Swiss cheese.*

Republican Palace: One of the Iraqi leader's seventy-eight ornate palaces, located on the banks of the Tigris River in Baghdad. It was destroyed during the 2003 Iraq War.

Tracers: A type of ammunition that leaves a trail of chemical smoke to mark the path of its flight.

Resound: Echo loudly.

Artillery: Large caliber, mounted weapons.

Mortars: Muzzle-loading cannons.

Strafing: Raking with machine-gun fire from low-flying aircraft.

A-10 Warthog: A low-flying U.S. military attack plane.

The noise is like nothing I've ever heard. I record it, but when I listen later, the result doesn't even begin to capture the reality....

[She talks to her editor on the phone.] As I get off the phone, there's a huge blast that literally throws me from my chair. The hotel shudders. I think another bomb has landed close by and continue typing. The hotel phone rings. It's **Amer.** I assume he wants to tell me about an upcoming press conference and I start to mutter that I'm about to go on the air when he interrupts with the words "Get out now. Hotel hit." I am struck by a rush of **adrenaline** and a surreal calm all at once. I have been anticipating something like this for too many days....

First there is relief that there doesn't seem to be much damage. There's no sign of any fire. Someone points to a chipped balcony on the 15th floor, four floors above my room. It doesn't look very bad. But then the **casualties** appear. Someone wrapped in a bloody sheet is carried out. Then another body. Everyone is desperately asking one another who's been hurt....

Most of us immediately assumed an Iraqi **irregular,** angered by Iraqi setbacks in the war and knowing the hotel housed foreign journalists, had taken a potshot at the building with a shoulder-launched, rocket-propelled grenade. However, a television camera had recorded the turn of a U.S. tank **turret,** its aim at the hotel, and the subsequent blast. News comes from the hospital: two cameramen have died. Three others remain in the hospital with wounds. The shell glanced off the balcony, spraying those standing in room 1502 with concrete and metal....

I can barely contain my anger, and the explanations coming out of **Central Command** in **Doha** do nothing to improve the situation. No one at the hotel saw or heard any outgoing fire. A spokesman says the soldiers didn't know the building they were aiming at was the Palestine, despite its distinctive architecture, and the well-known fact that just about every journalist in town is living and working here. For nearly three weeks, foreign reporters have operated with the gnawing fear that a so-called smart bomb or missile might **inadvertently** slam into our temporary home. It really didn't occur to anyone that the hotel in central Baghdad would be deliberately targeted by U.S. ground forces.

April 9, 2003

Silence is much noisier than the boom, boom of bombs. And that's what woke me today. The security guy in the hallway was

---

Amer: The name of Garrels's Iraqi assistant.

Adrenaline: A hormone that is released into the bloodstream when a person is excited.

Casualties: People killed or wounded in a war.

Irregular: A fighter that is not part of the formal armed forces.

Turret: A revolving structure containing guns on top of a tank.

Central Command: The U.S. military leaders in charge of troop movements during the Iraq War.

Doha: A city on the Persian Gulf in the nation of Qatar.

Inadvertently: Without realizing it; by mistake.

gone. I walked downstairs into the lobby at about 7 [o'clock]. It was empty, completely empty. All the people we have feared for so long have gone, evaporated. The **Information Ministry** is locked up....

If there is to be a last-ditch fight by the **Republican Guard**, Saddam's vaunted troops, or by **fanatical** irregular forces, they are nowhere to be seen today. In neighborhood after neighborhood the **Baath Party** members, steely-eyed security, and police have vanished. Iraqi troops have fled their sandbagged trenches. Under a bridge I saw surface-to-air missiles left unmanned. An army jacket and a pair of military boots lay strewn across an intersection. No one knew the fate of Saddam, but suddenly it didn't matter.

Reporters looking for U.S. troops tripped on them in the eastern suburbs, where they found themselves face to face with Abrams tanks. Marines moved quickly into abandoned Iraqi bunkers. Told there were no Iraqi military units anywhere between them and the city center, the Marine company commander reportedly chortled, "Love it, love it."

What has followed has been an **orgy** of looting. First there were just a few clusters of young men on the streets, but as people realized there was nothing stopping them anymore, the crowds grew, their fury focused on the symbols of Saddam's power. Groups broke into government buildings and warehouses, taking everything that wasn't nailed down and then some: chairs, air conditioners, computers, even doors. I see a yacht being pulled along downtown Sadoun Street.... Outside the **Oil Ministry**, a young man stands in front of a statue of Saddam imitating his grand gesture. A friend snaps a photo. Such a **lark** would have cost him his life just yesterday.

As more and more tanks lumber forward to the hotel, crowds begin to gather in nearby **Firdos Square**. A fifty-four-year-old taxi driver tosses his shoes at a statue of Saddam, a deeply insulting gesture in the Arab world. "We were surrounded by fear," he tells me. "Even fathers and sons were afraid to speak openly to each other." He recalls a friend who was arrested in 1978 and never seen again. "Thank you, America," he says, "for removing the dictator." He then joins a small group that tries to pull down the statue. After attempts with ropes and sledgehammers fail, the Marines move in a tank with a long boom to assist. The statue folds, falling to its knees, as the regime has.

The street scenes are nothing as joyous as the cameras make them out to be. There are plenty of people standing around, numb or shocked at the events. Dr. Sa'ad Jawad, an Iraqi political scientist, watches sadly as the Marines help topple Saddam's statue, calling the

Information Ministry: A building in downtown Baghdad that served as headquarters for the Iraqi government officials who dealt with foreign journalists.

Republican Guard: An elite, one hundred thousand-man force that was the best-trained and best-equipped part of Iraq's army.

Fanatical: Extreme devotion to a cause.

Baath Party: Iraq's ruling political party, which was led by Saddam Hussein.

Orgy: Widespread outbreak.

Oil Ministry: A building in downtown Baghdad that served as headquarters for the Iraqi government officials in charge of the petroleum industry.

Lark: Harmless mischief.

Firdos Square: The place in central Baghdad where a statue of Saddam Hussein was torn down on April 9, 2003, symbolizing the fall of the Iraqi regime.

Smoke rising over the Iraqi capital of Baghdad. A scene like this was not uncommon for Anne Garrels to witness and report on during the 2003 Gulf War. ©*Reuters NewMedia Inc./Corbis. Reproduced by permission.*

Resented: Met with feelings of anger or ill will.

Moscow in 1991: A reference to Garrels's coverage of the fall of communism in the former Soviet Union.

*scene humiliating. No fan of Saddam, he nonetheless warns of wounded pride. He acknowledges that now the Americans are here, they must be in full control, but he says their control will quickly be **resented.***

When I get back upstairs, Amer confesses that he wept as he watched the scene below. Though he too hated Saddam, he says seeing American troops in Baghdad is more than he can bear. He doesn't want their help.

*Pulling down statues makes for good television, but as I saw in **Moscow in 1991**, it doesn't ultimately signify much. It doesn't begin to answer the deeper questions. Wiping out the past doesn't mean coming to terms with it. That's what Amer is struggling with: Who are the Iraqis? How did they get a Saddam? How did they tolerate the fear Saddam created? And where do they go from here?*

What happened next...

Garrels returned to the United States a few days after Baghdad fell to U.S. troops. She was surprised at the impact her coverage of the war had on NPR's listeners. "I had been in a cocoon in Baghdad and had no idea what impact my reporting had had. I knew I was one of just a few [journalists] who had stayed, but I hadn't seen the e-mail from listeners," she said in the NPR interview. "It was both wonderful and alarming, and in a way I realized that I just needed to hide for a while and digest everything that had happened."

Garrels contacted a publisher and reached an agreement to write a book about her experiences. *Naked in Baghdad* was published in September 2003. The book covers her experiences in the Iraqi capital before, during, and after the war. Interspersed throughout the memoir are e-mail bulletins sent by her husband, the artist Vint Lawrence, updating friends around the world on Garrels's activities in Iraq.

On the strength of her reporting during the Iraq War, Garrels won the 2003 Courage in Journalism Award from the International Women's Media Foundation. She returned to Baghdad in the fall of 2003 to cover postwar security problems. "I think the postwar situation is really more dangerous in some ways than it was during the war," she explained in the NPR interview. "As the Iraqis predicted, it is a chaotic situation. Even those Iraqis who might have supported the ouster of Saddam Hussein predicted all along that there'd continue to be opposition to the Americans, that there would be Saddam loyalists, that the society would fracture along religious and tribal lines, which it has done."

Did you know...

- It took great courage for Garrels to remain in Baghdad for the duration of the war. After all, eighteen journalists were killed during the conflict, including two in the hotel where she was staying. She explained her reasons for staying in Baghdad in her book: "E-mails from listeners often raise the question, why do I do what I do? It's infinitely fascinating, is the crude answer. But I'm not really very interested in the strictly military part of war. Rather I'm fascinated by how people survive, and how the process of war affects the attitudes of all sides involved, and how they pull out of it."

- Garrels chose to call her book *Naked in Baghdad* for two reasons. First, she felt naked because she had no protection in the Iraqi capital during wartime. Second, she actually broadcast in the nude on her smuggled satellite telephone. "I broadcast naked in a sort of desperate effort to give myself a few extra minutes as the security goons went on their regular sweeps of the hotel looking for the illegal equipment that we had," she said in the NPR interview. "I figured that if I answered the door naked, I'd get a few minutes to shut the door, hide the phone, throw on a dress that I had laid out ready for such an event, and then let them in."

For More Information

"Anne Garrels: Foreign Correspondent." *NPR, 2003*. Available online at http://www.npr.org/about/people/bios/agarrels.html (last accessed on February 25, 2004).

Garrels, Anne. *Naked in Baghdad: The Iraq War as Seen by NPR's Correspondent*. New York: Farrar, Straus, and Giroux, 2003.

"A Special Q&A about *Naked in Baghdad*." *NPR, 2003*. Available online at http://www.npr.org/about/people/bios/agarrels_qa.html (last accessed on February 27, 2004).

George W. Bush

*Excerpt from his speech announcing the end
of major combat operations in Iraq*

**Delivered from the flight deck of the
USS *Abraham Lincoln* on May 1, 2003**

On May 1, 2003, President George W. Bush made a historic speech in which he announced that major combat operations in Iraq were over after forty-three days of fighting. The president chose to make the announcement in a dramatic fashion from the flight deck of the aircraft carrier USS *Abraham Lincoln*. The ship had been stationed in the Persian Gulf earlier, but it was sailing off the coast of California at the time of the speech. Bush was flown to the ship in the copilot's seat of a U.S. Navy S-3B Viking jet. He wore a flight suit that indicated his military rank as commander in chief. The bridge of the ship was decorated with a large banner reading "Mission Accomplished."

In his "aircraft carrier" speech, Bush praised the performance of U.S. and coalition troops in Iraq. He congratulated the members of the military for bringing freedom to the Iraqi people while also acknowledging that the coalition forces still had work to do in order to capture leaders of the former regime, locate hidden weapons, and reconstruct Iraq. But he claimed that the successful war effort was an important step in the war against terrorism.

Things to remember while reading the excerpt from President Bush's "aircraft carrier" speech:

President George W. Bush addressing the nation on the Iraq situation. ©*Reuters NewMedia Inc./Corbis. Reproduced by permission.*

- Bush reserves special praise for several aspects of the U.S. military performance in Iraq. For example, he mentions the ground forces' rapid advance to Baghdad, which he calls "one of the swiftest advances of heavy arms in history." The president also mentions the coalition's extensive use of precision-guided weapons. These weapons allowed the coalition forces to strike at Saddam Hussein's regime while minimizing civilian casualties and damage to Iraq's infrastructure.

- Bush accuses Hussein of building palaces for himself instead of hospitals and schools for the Iraqi people. By the time the 2003 war ended, coalition troops had found evidence that the regime used illegal oil sales to enrich itself in the decade following the 1991 Persian Gulf War. For example, several of Hussein's seventy-eight ornate palaces were built or rebuilt during this period, while millions of ordinary Iraqis were suffering hardships under United Nations economic sanctions (trade restrictions intended to punish a country for breaking international law).

- Bush calls the successful war in Iraq a victory in the global war against terrorism. But many listeners questioned this remark. They pointed out that there was no evidence of a connection between Saddam Hussein and the terrorists responsible for the attacks that struck the United States on September 11, 2001. As time passed, it also appeared unlikely that Iraq possessed any weapons of mass destruction that could have fallen into terrorist hands. Finally, some experts claimed that anger over the U.S. invasion and occupation of Iraq actually increased support for terrorist groups in the Arab world.

Excerpt from
President Bush's speech announcing
the end of major combat operations in Iraq

Major combat operations in Iraq have ended. In the battle of Iraq, the United States and our allies have **prevailed.** And now our coalition is engaged in securing and **reconstructing** the country.

In this battle, we have fought for the cause of **liberty** and for the peace of the world. Our nation and our coalition are proud of this accomplishment, yet it is you, the members of the United States military, who achieved it. Your courage, your willingness to face danger for your country and for each other made this day possible. Because of you our nation is more secure. Because of you the **tyrant** has fallen and Iraq is free.

Operation Iraqi Freedom was carried out with a combination of precision and speed and boldness the enemy did not expect and the world had not seen before. From distant bases or ships at sea, we sent planes and missiles that could destroy an enemy division or strike a single **bunker.** Marines and soldiers charged to Baghdad across 350 miles of hostile ground in one of the swiftest advances of heavy arms in history. You have shown the world the skill and the might of the American armed forces.

This nation thanks all of the members of our coalition who joined in a noble cause. We thank the armed forces of the United Kingdom, Australia, and Poland who shared in the hardships of war. We thank all of the citizens of Iraq who welcomed our troops and joined in the liberation of their own country. And tonight, I have a special word for **Secretary Rumsfeld,** for **General Franks,** and for all the men and women who wear the uniform of the United States: America is grateful for a job well done.

The character of our military through history, the daring of **Normandy,** the fierce courage of **Iwo Jima,** the decency and idealism that turned enemies into allies is fully present in this generation. When Iraqi civilians looked into the faces of our service men and women, they saw strength and kindness and good will. When I look at the members of the United States military, I see the best of our country and I am honored to be your **commander in chief.**

Prevailed: Succeeded or won.

Reconstructing: Rebuilding a country's infrastructure, government, and economy following a war.

Liberty: Freedom.

Tyrant: Extremely cruel or brutal ruler.

Bunker: A fortified underground structure.

Secretary Rumsfeld: Donald Rumsfeld, the U.S. Secretary of Defense during the Iraq War.

General Franks: Tommy Franks, the U.S. Army general who led coalition forces during the Iraq War.

Normandy: A region on the Atlantic coast of France that was the site of a U.S.-led Allied invasion during World War II (1939–45).

Iwo Jima: An island in the western Pacific that was the site of a major battle between U.S. and Japanese forces during World War II.

Commander in chief: Highest-ranking member of a military force; in the United States, the president is commander in chief of the military.

Fallen statues: For example, the statue of Saddam Hussein that was torn down in Baghdad's Firdos Square on April 9, 2003, symbolizing the fall of the Iraqi regime.

Culminating: Resulting or ending.

Casualties: People killed or wounded in a war.

Nazi Germany: Germany under the leadership of Adolf Hitler, which the United States helped defeat during World War II.

Imperial Japan: The Japanese empire during World War II, which the United States helped defeat.

Allied: A group of nations that opposed Nazi Germany, Japan, and Italy (known as the Axis Powers) during World War II.

Regime: Government or rule.

Civilians: People who are not part of a military force, including women and children.

Intimidation: Forcing people to obey out of fear.

Oppressors: Those who exert control through abuse of power.

Enslavement: The condition of slavery; being forced to work as slaves.

Dictator: A person who rules with absolute power.

Ideology: System of beliefs.

In the images of **fallen statues** we have witnessed the arrival of a new era. For a hundred years of war, culminating in the nuclear age, military technology was designed and deployed to inflict **casualties** on an ever-growing scale. In defeating **Nazi Germany** and **Imperial Japan, Allied** forces destroyed entire cities, while enemy leaders who started the conflict were safe until the final days. Military power was used to end a **regime** by breaking a nation. Today we have the greater power to free a nation by breaking a dangerous and aggressive regime.

With new tactics and precision weapons, we can achieve military objectives without directing violence against **civilians.** No device of man can remove the tragedy from war, yet it is a great advance when the guilty have far more to fear from war than the innocent.

In the images of celebrating Iraqis we have also seen the ageless appeal of human freedom. Decades of lies and **intimidation** could not make the Iraqi people love their **oppressors** or desire their own **enslavement.** Men and women in every culture need liberty like they need food and water and air. Everywhere that freedom arrives, humanity rejoices, and everywhere that freedom stirs, let tyrants fear.

We have difficult work to do in Iraq. We're bringing order to parts of that country that remain dangerous. We're pursuing and finding leaders of the old regime who will be held to account for their crimes. We've begun the search for hidden chemical and biological weapons, and already know of hundreds of sites that will be investigated.

We are helping to rebuild Iraq, where the **dictator** built palaces for himself instead of hospitals and schools. And we will stand with the new leaders of Iraq as they establish a government of, by, and for the Iraqi people. The transition from dictatorship to democracy will take time, but it is worth every effort. Our coalition will stay until our work is done and then we will leave, and we will leave behind a free Iraq.

The battle of Iraq is one victory in a war on terror that began on September the 11th, 2001, and still goes on. That terrible morning, 19 evil men, the shock troops of a hateful **ideology**, gave America and the civilized world a glimpse of their ambitions. They imagined, in the words of one terrorist, that September the 11th would be the beginning of the end of America.

By seeking to turn our cities into killing fields, terrorists and their allies believed that they could destroy this nation's resolve and force our retreat from the world. They have failed....

*The liberation of Iraq is a crucial advance in the campaign against terror. We have removed an ally of **Al Qaeda** and cut off a source of terrorist funding. And this much is certain: No terrorist network will gain weapons of mass destruction from the Iraqi regime, because the regime is no more....*

*Our war against terror is proceeding according to the principles that I have made clear to all. Any person involved in committing or planning terrorist attacks against the American people becomes an enemy of this country and a target of American justice. Any person, organization, or government that supports, protects, or **harbors** terrorists is **complicit** in the murder of the innocent and equally guilty of terrorist crimes. Any outlaw regime that has ties to terrorist groups and seeks or possesses weapons of mass destruction is a grave danger to the civilized world and will be confronted. And anyone in the world, including the **Arab world**, who works and sacrifices for freedom has a loyal friend in the United States of America....*

The advance of freedom is the surest strategy to undermine the appeal of terror in the world. Where freedom takes hold, hatred gives way to hope. When freedom takes hold, men and women turn to the peaceful pursuit of a better life. American values and American interests lead in the same direction. We stand for human liberty.

*The United States upholds these principles of security and freedom in many ways: with all the tools of diplomacy, law enforcement, **intelligence**, and **finance**. We are working with a broad coalition of nations that understand the threat and our shared responsibility to meet it. The use of force has been and remains our last resort. Yet all can know, friend and **foe** alike, that our nation has a mission: We will answer threats to our security, and we will defend the peace....*

*The war on terror is not over, yet it is not endless. We do not know the day of final victory, but we have seen the turning of the tide. No act of the terrorists will change our purpose, or weaken our resolve, or **alter** their fate. Their cause is lost; free nations will press on to victory.*

Al Qaeda: A radical Islamic terrorist group responsible for the September 11, 2001, terrorist attacks against the United States.

Harbors: Provides shelter or refuge to.

Complicit: Closely associated with or responsible for.

Arab world: The region of North Africa and the Middle East where the majority of people speak the Arabic language.

Intelligence: Information gathered through spying activities.

Finance: Monetary payments or assistance.

Foe: Enemy.

Alter: Change.

What happened next...

Bush's twenty-three-minute speech received an enthusiastic response on board the *Lincoln*. In fact, the president was interrupted twenty-four times by cheering, and he received several standing ovations. Many Americans who watched on tele-

A U.S. Army Bradley fighting vehicle moves into position near a burnt humvee following a rocket propelled grenade attack on American troops on August 7, 2003. Even though President Bush announced an end to major combat operations during his aircraft carrier speech, U.S. soldiers continued to face dangerous conditions in Iraq. *Photograph by Scott Nelson. Getty Images. Reproduced by permission.*

vision appreciated Bush's message and found his speech stirring. But the "aircraft carrier" speech did not receive universal praise.

Some critics suggested that Bush staged the speech in order to increase his own popularity and political power. They pointed out that the *Lincoln,* which was on its way home after ten months in the Persian Gulf, had been turned around and sent back out to sea so that the U.S. coastline would not be visible to TV cameras. Critics also complained about Bush's decision to be flown to the ship on a fighter jet. Although it provided dramatic news footage, the flight created a security risk for Bush and also cost the American taxpayers a considerable amount of money. It also was not necessary, since the *Lincoln* was only 30 miles from the U.S. Naval Base in San Diego, California, well within helicopter range.

Political opponents suggested that Bush's dramatic gesture was intended to distract people's attention from domestic problems such as high unemployment rates. "The

president's going out to an aircraft carrier to give a speech far out at sea," said Senator John Kerry, the 2004 Democratic candidate for president, "while countless Americans are frightened stiff about the economy at home."

Finally, some people felt that it was too early to announce the end of combat operations in Iraq. They questioned whether the U.S. military had really accomplished its mission. After all, Hussein and his sons had not been captured at that point, no evidence of weapons of mass destruction had been found, and no concrete plans for Iraq's future existed. Some analysts believed that reconstructing Iraq and forming a democratic government would be the most difficult tasks of all.

President George W. Bush meets with pilots and crew members of the aircraft carrier USS *Abraham Lincoln* before giving a speech to announce that major combat operations were over in Iraq. *Photograph by Hector Mata. AFP/Getty Images. Reproduced by permission.*

Did you know...
- Bush's landing on the *Lincoln* marked the first time in history that a sitting president arrived on the deck of an

aircraft carrier by plane (other presidents have traveled to the ships by helicopter). The four-seater S-3B Viking jet also carried two experienced navy pilots and a Secret Service agent. The jet made a "tailhook" landing, swooping down on the flight deck at 150 miles (241 kilometers) an hour, hooking a steel cable, and coming to a complete stop in less than 400 feet (122 meters).

- Before leaving Naval Air Station North Island in San Diego, California, Bush was briefed on what he would need to do to eject from the plane in case of emergency. Earlier, he also underwent water survival training in preparation for his flight.

- Bush was an F-102 fighter pilot in the Texas Air National Guard following his graduation from Yale University in 1968. Upon arriving on the *Lincoln,* he told reporters that he had taken the controls of the jet for about one-third of the trip.

- Analysts noted that Bush did not formally declare the Iraq War to be over in his "aircraft carrier" speech. Instead, he announced an end to major combat operations in Iraq. They believed that the president did this intentionally in order to keep his options open. Under international law, declaring the war to be over could complicate the coalition's efforts to track down former members of Hussein's regime. Coalition forces were still questioning thousands of Iraqi prisoners of war at that time, and declaring an end to the hostilities would have required the release of these prisoners.

For More Information

"Commander in Chief Lands on USS *Lincoln.*" *CNN.com,* May 2, 2003. Available online at http://www.cnn.com/2003/ALLPOLITICS/05/01/bush.carrier.landing/ (last accessed on February 27, 2004).

Purdum, Todd S., and the staff of the *New York Times. A Time of Our Choosing: America's War in Iraq.* New York: Times Books, 2003.

Salam Pax

Excerpt from his postwar Internet diary or "blog"

Collected in *Salam Pax:*
The Clandestine Diary of an Ordinary Iraqi, 2003

The 2003 Iraq War received more news coverage than any conflict in history. More than twenty-seven hundred journalists from news organizations and television networks around the world reported on the war. In addition to these traditional media outlets, the Internet emerged as an alternative source of news and information about the war. The World Wide Web allowed ordinary people from around the world to express their viewpoints and share their experiences during the war.

One of the most interesting accounts of the events in Iraq came from a mysterious figure who called himself Salam Pax (both first and last names mean "peace," in Arabic and Latin, respectively). Although Salam Pax kept his identity secret, he was eventually discovered to be a twenty-nine-year-old Iraqi architect who lived with his parents in a suburb of Baghdad. Beginning in September 2002, Salam Pax posted his thoughts and feelings to a weblog, or "blog" (an online diary that anyone can read on the Internet), at dear_raed.blog sport.com. The entries took the form of notes to his friend Raed, who was away studying for a master's degree in Jordan.

The early blog entries merely kept Raed informed about his friend's life. "The first two months were just: that girl got married, I had the flu.... Stupid stuff," Salam Pax told Rory McCarthy in an interview for *The Guardian*. "I never thought there would be this much of a fuss about the whole thing." But as he surfed the Internet, Salam Pax gradually realized that few other bloggers were writing in English about life in the Arab world. "All you saw was people talking about God and Allah," he related to McCarthy. "There was nothing about what was happening here." He came to believe that sharing an Iraqi perspective on the approaching war could be valuable.

From this point on, Salam Pax's blog focused on the events he saw taking place around him. He described the hardships of life in Iraq under Saddam Hussein's government. He talked about friends and relatives who had been arrested or executed for no apparent reason, and discussed how the Iraqi people lived in a constant state of paranoia and fear. Since Iraqis were not allowed to criticize Hussein in any way, Salam Pax took a huge risk in writing so candidly about the regime. In fact, he feared that the Iraqi intelligence agency might be after him on several occasions. "There was the possibility that they knew," he acknowledged in the *Guardian* interview. "I spent a couple of days thinking this is the end. And then you wait for a couple of days and nothing happens and you say, 'OK, let's do it again.' Stupid risks, one after the other."

Salam Pax's blog covered events leading up to the Iraq War, including its effect on his family. One day he helped his mother pack all of their valuables so they could leave town on a moment's notice. Another day he put tape around the edges of all the windows in the house to seal them in case of a poison gas attack. Once the war began, Salam Pax provided harrowing descriptions of the early days of the conflict, including the constant bombing of Baghdad. Unlike many Iraqis, he was able to watch some international news coverage of the war on television using his family's illegal satellite dish.

Salam Pax suddenly stopped posting to his blog on March 25, 2003. By this time, his personal account of the war had attracted thousands of dedicated readers around the world. His fans worried that he may have been killed or forced to go into hiding. As it turned out, Salam Pax was safe but had lost his Internet connection due to power outages in Baghdad. He continued keeping a diary of his experiences in a loose-leaf notebook for the remainder of the war. "After eight months, it became a habit," he explained to McCarthy.

Salam Pax finally resumed posting to his blog on May 7, which is the point where the following excerpt begins. He filled in the gap from the previous six weeks with information from his spiral notebooks. These entries described the fall of Baghdad to U.S. troops on April 9, and the lawlessness and looting that followed. In this excerpt, which covers events after the war ended, Salam Pax describes his mixed feelings about the conflict and the postwar U.S. military occupation of Iraq. Although he feels grateful to be liberated from Hussein's rule, he also feels resentful about the U.S. invasion of his country. He expresses deep concerns about the process of rebuilding Iraq and creating a new government.

Things to remember while reading the excerpt from Salam Pax's blog:

- Salam Pax's mixed feelings about the war were shared by many Iraqis. The majority of Iraqi citizens were glad to be rid of Saddam Hussein, and they were grateful for U.S. intervention in that respect. But the war itself was terrible and created hardships for the Iraqi people. Some resented the U.S. invasion and felt humiliated by the poor performance of Iraq's armed forces. Once the war ended, the chaos and lack of security that plagued many areas raised doubts about Iraq's future. As Salam Pax points out in his blog, the different feelings that Iraqis held about the U.S. troops depended largely on their own personal experiences.

- In his blog, Salam Pax describes some of the hardships facing the Iraqi people during the postwar period. For example, Iraq suffered from gas shortages, power outages, a lack of clean drinking water, and a high rate of unemployment.

- Salam Pax criticizes the U.S. civil administration (the agency responsible for overseeing Iraq's postwar reconstruction). He accuses the agency of being disorganized

In Baghdad, Iraqis wait in line for propane gas used for cooking. In his blog, Salam Pax describes how the Iraqi people face gas shortages, power outages, a lack of clean drinking water, and a high unemployment rate during the postwar period. *Photograph by Mario Tama. Getty Images. Reproduced by permission.*

and inconsistent in its approach to rebuilding Iraq and helping the Iraqi people form a democratic government. His feelings were echoed by many experts, who claimed that the Bush administration should have anticipated more of the problems it faced during the postwar period.

Excerpt from Salam Pax: The Clandestine Diary of an Ordinary Iraqi

Wednesday, 7 May 2003

War sucks big time. Don't let yourself ever be talked into having one waged in the name of your freedom. Somehow, when the bombs start dropping or you hear the sound of machine-guns at the end of your street, you don't think about your **"imminent liberation"** any more.

But I am sounding now like the taxi-drivers I have fights with whenever I get into one. Besides asking for outrageous fares (you can't blame them: gas prices have gone up ten times, if you can get it), they start grumbling and mumbling and at a point they would say something like "Well, it wasn't like the mess it is now when we had Saddam." This is usually my cue for going into rage-mode. We Iraqis seem to have very short memories or we simply block the bad times out. I ask them how long it took for us to get the electricity back again after the **last war**? Two years until things got to what they are now, after two months of war. I ask them how was the water? Bad. Gas for car? Non-existent. Work? Lots of sitting in street tea-shops. And how did everything get back? **Hussein Kamel** used to literally beat and whip people to do the impossible task of rebuilding.

Then the question that would shut them up: "So, dear Mr Taxi-Driver, would you like to have your Saddam back? Aren't we just really glad that we can now at least have hope for a new Iraq? Or are we Iraqis just a bunch of impatient fools who do nothing better than grumble and whine? Patience, you have waited thirty-five years for days like these, so get to working instead of whining." End of conversation.

The truth is, if it weren't for **intervention** this would never have happened. When we were watching the **Saddam statue being pulled down**, one of my aunts was saying that she never thought she would see this day in her lifetime.

BUT...

War. No matter what the outcome is, these things leave a trail of destruction behind them. There were days when the **Red Crescent** was begging for volunteers to help take the bodies of dead people off the city street and bury them properly. The hospital grounds have been turned to burial grounds. When the electricity went out and there was no way the bodies can be kept until someone comes and identifies....

Friday, 9 May 2003

American **civil administration** in Iraq is having a shortage of Bright Ideas. I keep wondering what happened to the months of

Imminent: Ready to take place.

Liberation: The act of releasing or setting free.

Last war: The 1991 Persian Gulf War.

Hussein Kamel: Former member of Saddam Hussein's government who was in charge of Iraq's weapons programs for many years.

Intervention: The U.S. decision to go to war to remove Saddam Hussein from power in Iraq.

Saddam statue being pulled down: A reference to the statue of Saddam Hussein that was toppled in central Baghdad's Firdos Square on April 9, 2003, symbolizing the end of the Iraqi regime.

Red Crescent: A Muslim organization that provides medical care and other assistance, similar to the Red Cross.

Civil administration: The U.S.-run agency in charge of Iraq's postwar reconstruction.

"preparation" for a "post-Saddam" Iraq. What happened to all these 100-page reports? Where is that **Dick Cheney** report? Why is every single issue treated like they have never thought it would come up? What's with the juggling of people and ideas about how to form that "**interim** government"? Why does it feel like they are using the let's-try-this, let's-try-that strategy? Trial and error on a whole country?...

Friday, 23 May 2003

[He helps an American journalist deliver two dozen pizzas to a unit of U.S. soldiers. He enjoys the experience, which makes him think about the mixed feelings many Iraqis have toward the troops.] It is difficult—a two-sided coin. On one side they are the U.S. army, invader/liberator (choose what you like), big guns, strange sounds coming out of their mouths. The other side has a person on it that in many cases is younger than I am, in a country he wouldn't put on his choice of destinations. But he has this uniform on, the big gun and those dark, dark sunglasses, which make it impossible to see his eyes. Difficult....

Friday, 30 May 2003

[He responds to an e-mail accusing him of minimizing the U.S. contribution to removing Saddam from power.] There is no way to "minimize" the contribution of the USA in removing Saddam. The USA waged a friggin' war! How could you "minimize" a war? I have said this before: if it weren't for the intervention of the US, Iraq would have seen Saddam followed by his sons until the end of time. But excuse me if I didn't go out and throw flowers at the incoming missiles....

Anyway. I don't really understand why among the 26 million Iraqis I have to explain everything clearly. Are you watching the news? Can't you see the spectrum of reactions people have to the American presence in Iraq?

I was at an **ORHA** press conference the other day (got in with someone who had a press pass) and the guy up there on the podium said in answer to a question, that probably the people who have had good encounters with the coalition forces were saying things are getting better and those who have had bad things happening to them were saying things are getting worse.

Dick Cheney: Vice president of the United States who led some studies about postwar reconstruction and administration of Iraq.

Interim: Temporary.

ORHA: Office of Reconstruction and Humanitarian Assistance, a team of two hundred U.S. government personnel, humanitarian workers, and Iraqi experts charged with overseeing postwar rebuilding efforts in Iraq.

Two U.S. soldiers on patrol in Iraq. As Salam Pax points out in his blog, many Iraqis have mixed feelings about American troops. *Patrick Baz/AFP/Getty Images. Reproduced by permission.*

It is still too early to make any judgments. I don't feel that I have an obligation to say all is rosy and well. Iraq is not the black hole it used to be and there are a **bazillion** *journalists here doing better than I can ever do—they have a press ID and they know how to deal with stuff.*

As to the question "why are you not documenting Saddam's crimes?" Don't you see that this is not the sort of thing that should be discussed lightly in a blog like this one. And what's with "document-

Bazillion: A slang term meaning a huge number.

Afghanistan: A country located on the outskirts of the Middle East that sheltered the radical Islamic leader Osama bin Laden and the terrorist group Al Qaeda, organizers of the September 11, 2001, terrorist attacks against the United States. The U.S. attacked Afghanistan in October 2001 as the first phase of the global war against terrorism.

Syria or Iran: Two Middle Eastern countries considered unfriendly to the United States which, like Iraq, the Bush administration accused of supporting terrorists and trying to develop weapons of mass destruction.

*ing"? Me, tiny, helpless Salam, documenting things that were going on for thirty years? Sorry to blow your bubble, but all I can do is tell you what is going on in the streets and if you think journalists are doing a better job of that then maybe you should go read them. One day, like in **Afghanistan**, those journalists will get bored and go write about **Syria or Iran**. Iraq will be off your media radar. Out of sight, out of mind. Lucky you, you will have that option. I have to live it.*

What happened next...

By the time the Iraq War ended, Salam Pax's blog had created a worldwide sensation. His Internet diary was hugely popular and received more links from other sites than any other blog on the Web. Fans appreciated his fresh, lively, funny, and fearless commentary on life in Iraq before, during, and after the war. Since foreign journalists had trouble convincing ordinary Iraqis to express their feelings, Salam Pax provided a unique perspective on the conflict. "It was the great irony of the war," Rory McCarthy wrote in *The Guardian.* "While the world's leading newspapers and television networks poured millions of pounds [British currency] into their coverage of the war in Iraq, it was the Internet musings of a witty young Iraqi living in a two-story house in a Baghdad suburb that scooped them all to deliver the most compelling description of life during the war."

The "Baghdad Blogger," as Salam Pax became known, received a great deal of coverage in the mainstream media. He was featured in the *New York Times, Los Angeles Times, New Yorker,* and *Guardian,* as well as on CNN, National Public Radio (NPR), and the British Broadcasting Corporation (BBC). Between his engaging writing style and the mystery surrounding his identity, Salam Pax was an object of both fascination and controversy. Some people doubted that he was real, and rumors abounded that he was actually an American CIA agent posing as an Iraqi. But other people felt that his diaries were too detailed and accurate to be fictional.

Once the war ended, several foreign journalists managed to track down Salam Pax using clues from his blog. He granted a few interviews under the condition that the reporters not reveal his true identity. Following his interview with Rory McCarthy, Salam Pax got a job writing a biweekly column for *The Guardian.* He also signed a lucrative agreement with a New York publisher to collect his blog entries in a book. *Salam Pax: The Clandestine Diary of an Ordinary Iraqi* was published in late 2003.

Did you know...

- Salam Pax learned to speak English while living in Vienna, Austria. He spent several years in the city during his childhood, when his businessman father worked there. He also lived there by himself for eight years while he studied architecture. He reluctantly returned to Baghdad in 1996 at the request of his parents.

- Salam Pax kept his identity secret because he feared that Saddam Hussein's security forces would arrest him. Even his family did not know what he was up to until they heard a news story about the "Baghdad Blogger" on the BBC. Salam Pax also fooled members of the media. He served as an interpreter for several British and American journalists during the war, but they did not uncover the full story behind his wartime activities until later.

- As the popularity of his blog increased, many people speculated about Salam Pax's identity and questioned his family connections. He resented suggestions that his comfortable middle-class parents must have been members of Saddam Hussein's Baath Party. In fact he credited his parents with teaching him to question authority. In response to one critic, he wrote:

  Do not assume, not even for a second, that because you read the blog you know who I am or who my parents are. You are being disrespectful to the people who have put the first copy of George Orwell's 1984 [a chilling novel about a world where the government controls all aspects of people's lives] in my hands—a heavy read for a 14-year-old with bad English. But that banned book started a process and gave me the impulse to look at the world I live in a different way.

For More Information

Eng, Paul. "War of Words on the Web." *ABCNews.com,* March 27, 2003. Available online at http://www.abcnews.go.com/sections/world/SciTech/iraq_warweb030326.html (accessed on March 2, 2004).

Maas, Peter. "Salam Pax Is Real." *The Slate,* June 2, 2003. Available online at http://slate.msn.com/id/2083847/ (accessed on March 2, 2004).

McCarthy, Rory. "Salam's Story." *The Guardian,* May 30, 2003. Available online at http://www.guardian.co.uk/g2/story/0,3604,966768,00.html (accessed on March 2, 2004).

Pax, Salam. *Salam Pax: The Clandestine Diary of an Ordinary Iraqi.* New York: Grove Press, 2003.

Where to Learn More

The following list focuses on works written for readers of middle school or high school age. Books aimed at adult readers have been included when they are especially important in providing information or analysis that would otherwise be unavailable.

Books

Al-Khalil, Samir. *Republic of Fear: The Inside Story of Saddam's Iraq*. Berkeley: University of California Press, 1989.

Al-Radi, Nuha. *Baghdad Diaries: A Woman's Chronicle of War and Exile*. New York: Vintage, 2003.

Alterman, Eric, and Mark J. Green. *The Book on Bush: How George W. (Mis)leads America*. New York: Viking, 2004.

Atkinson, Rick. *In the Company of Soldiers: A Chronicle of Combat*. New York: Holt, 2003.

Boyne, Walter J. *Operation Iraqi Freedom: What Went Right, What Went Wrong, and Why*. New York: Forge, 2003.

Cipkowski, Peter. *Understanding the Crisis in the Persian Gulf*. New York: John Wiley, 1992.

Cronkite, Walter. *LIFE: The War in Iraq*. New York: Time Life Books, 2003.

Editors of *Time* Magazine. *21 Days to Baghdad: Photos and Dispatches from the Battlefield.* New York: Time Life Books, 2003.

Foster, Leila M. *The Story of the Persian Gulf War.* Chicago: Children's Press, 1991.

Frum, David. *The Right Man: The Surprise Presidency of George W. Bush.* New York: Random House, 2003.

Garrels, Anne. *Naked in Baghdad: The Iraq War as Seen by NPR's Correspondent.* New York: Farrar, Straus, and Giroux, 2003.

Goldschmidt, Arthur. *A Concise History of the Middle East.* Boulder, CO: Westview Press, 1989.

Haskins, James. *Colin Powell: A Biography.* New York: Scholastic, 1992.

Katovsky, Bill, and Timothy Carlson. *Embedded: The Media at War in Iraq.* Guilford, CT: Lyons Press, 2003.

Kent, Zachary. *George Bush.* Chicago: Children's Press, 1993.

Kent, Zachary. *The Persian Gulf War: The Mother of All Battles.* Hillside, NJ: Enslow, 1994.

King, John. *The Gulf War.* New York: Dillon Press, 1991.

Lehr, Heather. *The Kurds.* Philadelphia: Chelsea House, 2003.

Miller, Judith, and Laurie Mylroie. *Saddam Hussein and the Crisis in the Gulf.* New York: Times Books, 1990.

Moore, Robin. *Hunting down Saddam: The Inside Story of the Search and Capture.* New York: St. Martin's, 2004.

NBC Enterprises. *Operation Iraqi Freedom: The Inside Story.* New York: NBC, 2003.

Pax, Salam. *Salam Pax: The Clandestine Diary of an Ordinary Iraqi.* New York: Grove Press, 2003.

Pimlott, John. *Middle East: A Background to the Conflicts.* New York: Franklin Watts, 1991.

Purdum, Todd S., and the staff of the *New York Times.* *A Time of Our Choosing: America's War in Iraq.* New York: Times Books, 2003.

Rai, Milan. *War Plan Iraq.* London: Verso, 2002.

Renfrew, Nita. *Saddam Hussein.* New York: Chelsea House, 1992.

Richie, Jason. *Iraq and the Fall of Saddam Hussein.* Minneapolis: Oliver Press, 2003.

Ridgeway, James. *The March to War.* New York: Four Walls Eight Windows, 1991.

Rivera, Sheila. *Operation Iraqi Freedom.* Edina, MN: Abdo, 2004.

Rivera, Sheila. *Rebuilding Iraq.* Edina, MN: Abdo, 2003.

Rooney, Ben. *The Daily Telegraph War on Saddam: The Complete Story of the Iraq Campaign.* London: Robinson, 2003.

Ryan, Mike. *Baghdad or Bust: The Inside Story of Gulf War II.* Yorkshire, UK: Leo Cooper, 2003.

Salzman, Marian, and Anne O'Reilly. *War and Peace in the Persian Gulf: What Teenagers Want to Know.* Princeton, NJ: Petersen's Guides, 1991.

Sasson, Jean P. *The Rape of Kuwait: The True Story of Iraq's Atrocities against a Civilian People.* New York: Knightsbridge, 1991.

Scheer, Christopher. *The Five Biggest Lies Bush Told about Iraq.* New York: Akashic Books, 2003.

Sciolino, Elaine. *The Outlaw State: Saddam Hussein's Quest for Power and the Gulf Crisis.* New York: John Wiley, 1991.

Sifry, Micah L., and Christopher Serf, eds. *The Iraq War Reader.* New York: Simon and Schuster, 2003.

Steloff, Rebecca. *Norman Schwarzkopf.* New York: Chelsea House, 1992.

White, Thomas E., et al. *Reconstructing Eden: A Comprehensive Plan for the Postwar Political and Economic Development of Iraq.* Houston: Country Watch, 2003.

Videos and DVDs

CNN Presents: The War in Iraq—The Road to Baghdad. Wea Corp, 2003.

National Geographic: 21 Days to Baghdad. Warner Home Video, 2003.

Nightline: War against Iraq Begins. Mpi Home Video, 2001.

21st Century Guide to Operation Iraqi Freedom. U.S. Department of Defense, 2003.

War in the Desert. Red Distribution, Inc., 2003.

Web Sites

"Fog of War." *Washington Post.* Available at http://www.washington-post.com/wp-srv/inatl/longterm/fogofwar/fogofwar.htm (last accessed on May 13, 2004).

Frontline: The Gulf War. Available at http://www.pbs.org/wgbh/pages/frontline/gulf (last accessed on May 13, 2004).

Gulf Hello. Available at http://www.persiangulf.com (last accessed on May 13, 2004).

Gulf War.com. Available at http://www.gulfwar.com (last accessed on May 13, 2004).

Gulf War Index. Available at http://www.britains-smallwars.com/gulf/index.html (last accessed on May 7, 2003).

"The New Iraq." PBS *Online NewsHour.* Available at http://www.pbs.org/newshour/bb/middle_east/iraq/index.html (last accessed on May 13, 2004).

"War in Iraq." *CNN.com.* Available at http://www.cnn.com/SPECIALS/2003/iraq/index.html (last accessed on May 13, 2004).

Index

Bold type indicates main
entries and their page
numbers. Illustrations are
marked by (ill.)